Keep Calm and Cope With Grief

9 Chapters for Managing Fear and Grief When Losing a Parent or Loved One

John Allen

Table of Contents

To Mum (Nandy), who has taught me to cherish life and be the best man I can be. To my sister, Gillian, who has always been there for me and helped keep me out of trouble. To my daughter, Jessica, who is far wiser than her years and truly is an Earth Angel. To my Dog, Amadeus, who passed away during the writing of this book. Amo, you are my little brother, my best friend. I will miss you until the day I die, and then we'll be together again. And finally, to my fiancé, Alison. Without her love, support, and understanding, this book would have never been written. I love you, my queen!

Introduction

- Has your loved one recently been diagnosed with an incurable disease?
- Have you had to say final goodbyes to a loved one?

Dealing with the loss or imminent loss of a loved one is never easy. The one staying behind is filled with so many emotions, including guilt, remorse, anger, and heartache. No two people will express or have the same emotions. Friends, family, and strangers would tell me that they knew how I felt and what I was going through, but did they actually?

The Window Into My World

I was born and raised in Liverpool, a working-class city in England in the United Kingdom. When I was growing up, money was sparse in Liverpool, but it didn't seem to affect the citizens or my family. What they lacked in wealth was made up for with an abundance of kindness, enormous senses of humor, and the selfless willingness to help others. Something that has never changed, and I doubt it ever will, is that the citizens of my childhood hometown are very witty with a hint of sarcasm. Now, if you don't know Liverpudlians, you might just mistake their way of life as being rude and insensitive. Trust me, that is not their intention. Everyone loves to make fun of each other and they know not to take anything too seriously—unless it's about soccer (European football)! The English take their soccer very seriously; therefore, it is best (and safer) to keep your opinions about the various clubs to yourself.

My Family

My parents, my rocks, and my foundations were and are still two of the most amazing people in my life. My upbringing was based on the traditional old-school ways. Dad worked Mondays to Fridays from 9 a.m. until 6 p.m. Mum stayed at home to take care of me and my sister. Dad was always the stricter parent and we knew not to step out of line. I would never have dared to fake being ill to take a day off school. Dad would have seen through the veil, which would have resulted in my hide being tanned and hung out on a flagpole for all of Liverpool to see.

As I have mentioned, I do have a sister, and she is five years younger than me. As we were growing up, Mum got herself a part-time job. It was good for her to get out of the house for a couple of hours a day, and, as a bonus, she was able to earn a couple of extra pounds. Money was always tight for our family, as well as many other families in Liverpool, but that never affected us. I can tell you one thing, though; we never went without. We had food on the table, a roof over our heads, a warm bed to sleep in, and clothes to wear.

As I reflect on my childhood during this difficult period of my life, I realize that I was very privileged growing up. I would even go so far as to say that I was spoiled! Yes, I grew up wearing hand-me-down clothes and shoes. I never owned a pair of brand-new jeans until I was 15 years old! But I never once felt that I was missing out or that I was being deprived of anything. There were always presents under the Christmas tree and birthday presents set out on the table on these special days. School holidays were always a treat because we'd pack a picnic and spend the day at the beach, or we would drive to Cornwall and spend a couple of weeks on a farm near the coast.

I have a fairly large family, which is made up of 12 aunts and uncles, and between them, they have gifted me with 21 cousins. As far as growing our family, most of my cousins have gotten married and have had children themselves. Family celebrations were never in short supply, and we celebrated many christenings, weddings, birthdays, and milestones together. I think it is safe to say that we would create an event as an excuse so that we could all get together to celebrate something at any given time.

I have so many memories and stories that have been imprinted in my mind. Our family was made up of great memories of all the wonderful times we got to spend together. I enjoy sitting around the fire pit with friends and loved ones and reminiscing about all the shenanigans we got up to during our childhood. There is just something so special about sharing memories with friends and family that transports you back in time to the setting you are remembering.

Looking to the Future

I would always think about my future when I was growing up. No matter which stage of my life I was in, I knew for certain that I wanted to do something to make my parents proud. I was constantly thinking how disappointed my parents would be if I made wrong choices or came home with poor grades. I struggled with low confidence and self-esteem, which was part of me wanting to be perfect in everything I set out to do. As a young adult, I was afraid that I would fail in everything that I set out to do or that I would not measure up to the expectations of everyone around me.

It was at that point when life knocked at my door, stepped in, and helped me decide to make a life-altering change. I was about 26 years of age at that point. I packed up my life and left Liverpool. Life has a funny way of intervening when we sit on the fence and cannot decide which direction to move into when we have difficulty making decisions or expressing our concerns.

I might have moved away from Liverpool, but returning to my childhood home was extra special. The moment I would step foot into my childhood home, I would immediately feel the outpouring of love, caring, and friendship from my loved ones. Home is where the heart is, and no matter where in the world you live, you will always find comfort where your loved ones reside. I may be living in another country and I might have a new life, but going back to Liverpool is a treasured gift that I will carry with me for all eternity.

In February 2020, Dad reached out to me to tell me that he had been diagnosed with cancer. I was devastated that my rock, the strongest person I knew, had informed me that he didn't have long to live. Dad was meant to outlive everyone. My world started spinning uncontrollably because Dad kept me on the right track in life. He guided me and showed me how to respect the girls I dated. He helped with the career paths I pursued. In short, Dad was my best friend, always there when I needed someone to talk to, and someone I could share anything with.

My World Imploded

The news of Dad's cancer diagnosis brought me to my knees. I cried for two days straight. I was exhausted. I didn't want to accept that he was about to enter the next phase of his life. I wasn't ready for him to leave me. Yes, I was being selfish. I wanted him to stay and share more of his wisdom with me. It wasn't meant to be because Dad left this earth on November 23rd, 2o2o surrounded by his loved ones.

It was at that point that I realized just how short and precious life is. I don't believe anyone understands what grief and pain feel like until they are in a position where they have lost someone close to them. You develop a new sense of feelings and you appreciate the love you have for those closest to you. You also develop the sense of feeling something you have never wanted to feel before—pain. A pain that no medication can take away. Confronting and dealing with this new feeling of pain is one of the hardest challenges you will ever have to experience. That is where I was, and where I still am. I am getting better because I have learned to embrace life and not take anything for granted.

Find the Light

How easy life would be if we could be protected from feeling pain. Grief doesn't discriminate who it will attach itself to. Grief doesn't care what your religion or religious denomination is. Grief doesn't care about your gender. Oh no, grief is like a thief that swoops in and punches you in the gut, bruises your heart with its powerful grip, and fills your tear ducts with an endless supply of water. It can steal your breath and suck you into a vacuum. Grief can make you do things you never would have thought of otherwise. It can lead you down dark alleyways. Grief is something that can stay with you for a lifetime and it can hold you hostage—if you allow it to.

I am here to tell you that you can break free from the grips of grief. It is okay to carry on living your life. Your loved ones will always be in your heart, and even when the memories begin to fade, their love for you will remain imprinted in your heart and mind. Honor your loved ones by going out there and enjoying life. No one would ever want you to sit in darkness and grieve for the rest of your time on this earth.

I want this book to be a beacon of light to you in your time of darkness. I hope that this book will soften the pain you are feeling. I hope that you will continue along this journey with me as we learn to understand that life has to go on and that loss doesn't have to hurt so much. Together we will embark on this journey that will teach us some healing skills and coping techniques. We're going to learn that we are never going to be alone and that we will always have someone watching over us and walking beside us. Our loved ones might be gone from our sight but never from our hearts and minds.

We are going to learn that it is perfectly normal to have excellent days where laughter bubbles out of our souls or sad days where sights, sounds, and/or smells trigger memories that open up a cascade of tears. The loss of a loved one, whether a friend, a spouse/partner, a family member, or a beloved pet is something we all have to experience at some point during our lifetime. Look forward to the days when we will be reunited with our loved ones. Your loved ones may be gone from your sight but they will always remain in your memories.

Chapter 1:

The Reality of Losing a Loved

One

Nobody wants to think about the possibility of saying farewell to their parents, loved ones, or friends. We want to believe that death is for everyone else, not the people in your close circle. Death is not something anyone wants to think about, let alone prepare for.

- How does someone deal with the news that their loved ones are going to leave this earth?
- How are you meant to prepare for something so final?
- How does anyone know when it is the right time to crack a smile or laugh?

I am not a fortune teller, so I cannot tell you how you should be feeling. I also cannot tell you what you should be doing. Everyone experiences and copes with loss in their unique ways. What worked for Jared and Brittney may not work for you. So no, I'm not going to tell you what kinds of emotions you should be experiencing or what processes you need to follow. What I am going to be doing is giving you various ideas and tips on what you *could* be doing to help you through the process.

I want you to know that you are going to experience emotions you have never felt before. Never hold back or suppress your feelings or emotions. You don't have to hold it together all the time. I get that you want to be strong for everyone else, but don't ever forget that you need to mourn as well. This is a journey you are going to want to embark on. You will want to know as much information as possible. You will want to be prepared—to a point. Friends, it is okay to experience all the feelings you have. Let them out. Find a release. Death is something we all have to deal with at some point. Make the most of all the todays because tomorrow is not guaranteed.

Earth-Shattering News

- What do you do when you find out that your loved one is dying?
- How does the news make you feel?
- What should you be doing for your loved one?
- What are your loved one's expectations after they leave this earth?
- What happens when you are in denial and don't believe your loved one's time on this earth is running out?

When Dad let me know in February 2020 that he had been diagnosed with cancer and that he was dying, I was at a loss. Firstly, I was living in the United States of America and Dad was in the United Kingdom. Secondly, we were living in unprecedented times where a global pandemic was dictating our lives, as well as preventing international travel. Thirdly, I was in shock and didn't know whether I was Arthur or Martha. All I knew was that my world was spinning out of control and that Dad had been given a death sentence. I *needed* to get to him.

My fiancé and I jumped through numerous hoops to get back to Liverpool. As mentioned, it was extremely difficult to fly during the pandemic, but we got there. I was able to spend an unforgettable week with Dad. I do find myself thinking back to the week I spent with Dad and asking myself many questions. In the moment, when you are with your loved one, you do tend to have some kind of mental block where you don't want to think about the future. All you really want is to allow those special moments to become imprinted in your mind. I have mentioned it before, and I will, in all likelihood, repeat it a couple more times, but not everyone will have the same experience during the death and grieving process of a loved one.

Some people will cry, and others will not. It is not a reflection on you, as a person, of how you felt about your loved one. Some people will express anger and may very well take out their frustrations on those closest to them. Some people will experience shock and onlookers will mistake that for a lack of caring. Let me tell you that grief has no timestamp. Grief won't give you a warning of when it will knock you down. Grief is something that will blow your socks off when you least expect it.

- Can you prepare for grief?
- Can you schedule in when you would like grief to make an appearance?

The short answer is *no*! The long answer is, various coping skills can help you before the time. These coping skills won't block out any feelings, but they can help you with the transition.

Your Loved One Is Dying

This is by far one of the most traumatic times you will ever encounter. Your emotions are on overdrive and you're feeling overwhelmed. You are preparing to watch someone you love with every fiber of your being slip away from life. If you are like billions of other people who have access to the internet, you have most probably searched for the illness or disease to see what it's all about. You may have spoken to many doctors, surgeons, and specialists, but you wanted to find holes in their diagnosis. It doesn't matter that you don't have a medical degree, Google is more knowledgeable than anyone with a degree, right? No, sorry, Google doesn't have a degree in anything except filling you with more anxiety than you need.

I've had many people tell me that I was lucky to have been given the time to say goodbye to Dad. I do realize that many people don't get that opportunity and it is a case of: one moment they were there and in the blink of an eye, they were gone. My heart goes out to everyone who has lost a loved one. I wouldn't wish it on my worst enemy. And yes, I was lucky to have had that special time with Dad. When the time came for us to return to the United States, I started asking myself many questions. It was then that I realized that there are no right or wrong answers or scenarios. Confused? Let me give you a rundown of the moment realization kicked in.

Keep Calm

The first and most important thing you need to do is remain calm. Yes, your world has imploded. Yes, your loved one has been diagnosed with a life-threatening disease. The second thing you should *not* be doing is running ahead of the train to plan the funeral of something that is still with you. No one knows when the end will come, and for all you know, your loved one will live anywhere from a couple of days and weeks to months or years. I know that it is easy for someone to tell you to stay calm when you have been dealt with devastating news. What we don't think about is that we are all going to pass away at some point.

Enjoy Quality Time

Your loved one knows that their days on earth are numbered. They have more than likely made peace with the news. They are even more than likely being brave for you because they can see the fear in your eyes when you are with them. I know what it is like to put on a cheerful smile and brave face when all you want to do is hug your loved one and sob into their shoulder. Show them how much they mean to you. Pick a flower from the garden to give to them. Ask them what they want to do. Don't think you know what your loved ones want; let them tell you what they want or need from you. Enjoy your time together and treat each moment as if it is the last. Remember what I said earlier—tomorrow is not guaranteed.

Who's the Boss?

Your loved ones are in control of their lives. They may be ill and they might be dying, but they can make decisions. Don't try to sway their minds or make choices for them. Allow them the dignity of making choices for the future of their spouse, partners, children, or charities. They don't need you to put pressure and undue stress on them. Rather, show them your support and help them. The choices and decisions being made might not be what you would like, but it is not your life. If your loved one doesn't want a funeral, don't go planning one because that is going against their wishes. If your loved one wants to be cremated and their ashes scattered somewhere, don't have a burial. A little bit of compassion, help, and understanding will go a very long way.

Acceptance

This is a very difficult part of the process. Acceptance is the gift of understanding that you will be reunited with your loved one. We have to understand, whether we want to or not, that death is something that is going to happen whether we are ready for it or not. We don't get to decide when we leave this world because it has already been chosen for us. We are on loan to this world. When our purpose and destiny have been fulfilled and we have done what was needed to be done, we have to answer the call to leave this world.

In Perspective: It's Not About You

You will go into fight or flight mode when you are informed of your loved one's diagnosis. You don't want to believe that their lives are ending. A part of you always knew that death was a possibility. Another part of you is and will never be ready to face that possibility. Denial has a way of obscuring reality. No one ever wants to think about death and it is easier to ignore it. Unfortunately, death doesn't require denial's permission to take your loved one.

It is important to understand why death has to happen. Oh, you can ignore it, but that will only make it harder for you when the time arrives. I know that the news is devastating to you as a child, a spouse, a partner, or a parent. It is difficult to wrap your mind around the news that you have received and your instincts are to rush in and be the hero. Nothing can stop you from trying to fix things up, but stop, take a deep breath, and take a look at your loved one.

- What do they want?
- What is their expression telling you?
- What are their eyes trying to convey to you?
- What are they saying to you?

What Happens When You Realize It's Not About You?

The process of acceptance will be easier to cope with when you allow reality to take the center stage. Accept that you cannot change a diagnosis. Don't spend the time fighting with acceptance when you could be spending quality time with your loved one. Make your peace with acceptance and send denial packing. You are not meant to be the glue that holds everyone and everything together. I have it on good authority that you are not a robot and that if you prick your finger it will bleed. That is one of the most obvious signs that you are allowed to accept what is happening to your loved one.

- You will feel the pain of losing your loved one.
- You will experience emotions you never thought were possible.
- You will feel a wave of anger that you never knew existed.
- You will feel relief.
- You will feel sadness.
- You will feel regret.

In Perspective: Talk and Listen

There will be times when you want to talk about how you are feeling. There may be times when you are going to clam up and not want to speak to anyone. You might just want to be left alone with your feelings. There are no right or wrong ways to deal with grief and each person has their toolkit of coping techniques.

I found that I needed to communicate with family and friends. They needed to know that I was there for them, and vice versa. There would be days when I didn't want to speak and I clammed up. There were days when I talked and talked and half expected my sister or my fiancé to tell me to put a lid on it, but they never did. There were days when Mum and I would talk and laugh over memories. There were days when Dad and I would have discussions about his expectations. The most important thing is that no two people are alike and no two days will be the same. I would like nothing more than to rewind the time to when Dad was still with us. Reality stings at the best of times.

If you have been through a loss, you will recognize the importance of letting go and accepting support from friends, family, or even strangers. Reach out to someone in your community that is going through a loss. Be that person who can offer the support that is needed to understand why it is happening. Don't be that person that listens and turns the conversation to reflect on themselves. You will be humbled by the experience of being a support guide to someone who is experiencing a loss.

Your Loved One Has Passed On

The time has arrived when your loved one has departed from this world. It is undoubtedly one of the worst days you will ever experience. I was lucky—as lucky as someone could be in this situation—that I made it back to Dad's bedside before he exhaled his final breath. Not everyone is that lucky because, as I have already mentioned, death does not have a schedule that shows you a day, date, or time when it will come.

The days that follow will have you feeling as if you are living in a trance. You know what is going on around you, and you know that people are entering and leaving your home, but it sort of feels as if you are on the outside of a snow globe and looking in. Guess what? You're in shock. You know what happened, you understand why it happened, but yet you find yourself staring at your old friend, Mr. Denial, again. You keep expecting to wake up, but you don't.

Someone recently shared their experience of losing a loved one with me. In the days following the sudden death of the loved one, a family member took over all the arrangements and arranged for "babysitters" to be there every moment of every day for two weeks. This person didn't want to be coddled, kept company, or watched over for fear of self-harming. All this person wanted was to be alone. They wanted the space and freedom to mourn—alone. This person turned to work to help them cope with their loss. Their mind was kept busy so that they didn't have to think and obsess about what had happened.

Now I know you are thinking that this is unhealthy, but it worked for this person. They took their time to mourn when they were alone. They implemented coping techniques that worked for them. People were still calling and dropping in daily, but soon, the message was received loud and clear, and that was to give them space and time to mourn, cope, and heal without being pressured. One thing they did remember was a phone call from a friend who said: "Whatever you do, don't go dark and disappear from the world." That was a loaded statement that would serve as a reminder to everyone who is experiencing a loss, and that is that you should always be looking for the light.

My Story: Part 1

On the 20th of November, I received an email from my sister telling me that Dad was dying and that I needed to get back to Liverpool as soon as yesterday! I frantically scoured the airline websites for the earliest flight to England. I had found out eight months earlier that Dad had incurable cancer. I had known that the chances of survival were slim to none. Getting the news from my sister to come home did not prepare me for the fact that Dad's battle was nearing the end.

I booked a flight, packed a bag, and the next day I was flying from the United States to England. My travel experience could be described as the *Planes, Trains, and Automobiles* type of journey. Upon landing in London, I had to take a train to Lime Street Station in Liverpool. My brother-in-law Stephen and my nephew Matthew picked me up at the station in their car. The five-mile drive to Mum and Dad's house seemed to take forever. I had no idea whether I would get there in time.

We walked into the house around 1 p.m. and I immediately went upstairs to Dad's bedroom. I found him sitting up in his bed and watching an old western (he had always wanted to be a cowboy). The first words he uttered when he saw me were, "What are you doing here? I'm not ready yet." I knew what it meant, and he knew that me being there was a sign that the end was very close for him. I climbed onto the bed to hug him. Right now, I feel regret because I wish I'd never let go of him, but I realize now that it would have been selfish of me. I eventually settled down and we started talking. I realized as we were talking that he wasn't dying just yet. Everyone was running ahead of that train I mentioned. I told myself that he'd be okay and that we would have Christmas today. After all, it was only November 21st. I called my fiancé in the States, and I told her the good news that Dad was doing well.

How wrong was I? The local nurses had been there that afternoon and set up a hospital bed in my old bedroom. They moved Dad over and made him more comfortable. I slept on Mum and Dad's bedroom floor that night. At around 2 a.m., Mum came running in and woke me. Dad was throwing up and she needed help. We sat him up in the bed to make it easier for him to be sick. Dad was in so much pain and it was heart-wrenching to see him like that. He began to relax after a while and settled down to sleep again. I went back to the other room to try and get some rest, but within the hour, Mum woke me up again because Dad was throwing up. It happened every hour throughout the night.

It occurred to me that I should have called Gillian, my sister, to come over, but I figured that when Dad threw up, it would be the same process of getting him cleaned up, comfortable, and settled down so he would go back to sleep. The following morning when the local nurses visited, we shared what had happened during the night. All they could say was "it's normal." I felt the anger bubbling up inside of me because I wanted the nurses to do more. Yes, Dad was comfortable. Yes, he slept most of the morning and that afternoon. The television was on, but he wasn't interested.

We would place a wet sponge on his lips to make sure he didn't become dehydrated. We pressed a cold, damp cloth on his forehead. Mum, Gillian, and I sat around his bed talking to him about anything, everything, and nothing. At one point during our vigil, Dad woke up, reached out, and grabbed Mum's hand. He turned and looked at her and said: "We did alright, Nandy, didn't we? We did alright." And he went back to sleep. This is a memory that has been imprinted in my mind, one never to be forgotten. We stayed with Dad throughout the day. He was never alone that day.

We held his hand while he slept, brushed his hair, rubbed his feet, and took extra gentle care of the man who brought us so much joy and safety in our lives. I'm pretty sure Dad knew he was not alone because we were chatting up a storm around his bed as he dozed. I know that Dad will never be alone. I found myself wishing that Jessica, my daughter, and Alison, my fiancé, could have been there with us and shared in these special moments. Mum and I stayed with Dad that night. He had a peaceful night's rest with no throwing up and no drama. We managed to get some rest that night.

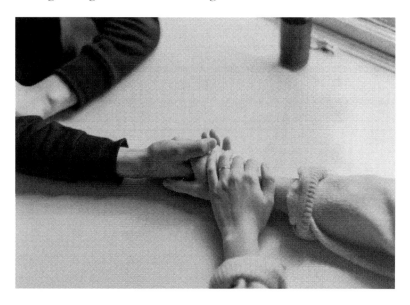

The next morning, which would also be Dad's last morning with us, he drifted in and out of sleep. Mum and Gillian went downstairs at one point to make a cup of tea and I stayed with Dad. I held his hand while he slept. I started scanning his body, trying to remember as much as I could. I looked at his veins. I looked at every single one of his freckles on his arm. I broke down and the floodgates were opened. He woke up and looked at me.

"Son, why are you crying?"

"Because I love you so much, Dad! I need you!" I replied.

His response to me was, "I love you, too, Son, but please don't cry or you'll get me crying, too." And then he went back to sleep. I don't believe he ever spoke again.

Later that afternoon, Mum, Gillian, her husband Stephen, their children Matthew and Rosie, and I stood around Dad's bed. We watched every breath and every movement. I think we might even have held our breaths so that we could listen to Dad's breathing. The nurses were in and out several times that afternoon to monitor Dad. One of the senior nurses informed us that Dad's breathing had slowed down and that his time to depart was very close. Within minutes, his departure time presented itself. At 19:26, Dad took his last breath.

I can still see that scene when I close my eyes. I can still hear the sobs coming from Mum and Gillian. I can still smell those hospital sheets on his bed. I've never seen death before that moment, and I can tell you right now, I never want to see it again. I wanted to reach out and bring Dad back. I wanted to trade places with Dad. I wanted to go instead of him. My grief was immediate. I asked myself why he had to be the one to leave. This wasn't fair. Life wasn't fair. Dad was only 79 years old. How did it come to this point? I was angry. I felt alone. I know that Dad is now pain-free and he has staked a piece of heaven for us when it is our turn to join him. My anger turned to confusion at my reaction. Why was I so angry when Dad was at peace?

I knew that the pain I felt that day, at that moment, would never go away. It had completely changed me. Ironically, thinking about it now reminds me of when Jessica was born. I was a changed man. I was a father. From a new life to the passing of a life. It is moments like this that change you forever.

Reflections From a Mourning Son

As I'm writing this and remembering the events as they played out that day, I am still brought to tears. The pain of losing a loved one never truly goes away. It's been just over a year, and I still feel numb. Multiple people have suggested that I should write or journal about my experience. I thought they were crazy. That is, until I started writing. Yes, I am reliving every moment of the last eight months of Dad's life, and yes, it is a pain I wouldn't wish on anyone, but writing and sharing my experience might help someone else who is having a difficult time coping. Writing is a way to remember the memories that were shared. Writing is a way to lock in those memories you are afraid to forget. Writing is a gentle reminder of how you can heal your heart, soften the pain, and help others who have not had the opportunity to grieve the way they needed to. Writing is therapeutic.

Chapter 2:

A Whole New World

I expected the world to stop for a moment, you know, as a sign of respect for Dad's passing and our loss. Boy, was I mistaken. Our world crashed before our eyes and the rest of the world went about their day without batting an eye. One could say that Mum, Gillian, and I were on autopilot for the first couple of days after Dad's death. We experienced a myriad of emotions which ranged from being strong in front of others and crumbling when alone to feeling useless and tearful.

The initial days following Dad's death went by in a blur. A year on and I am only now remembering more details. Writing about my experience is helping me more than I ever realized. I realized that a world without Dad would be a new normal for me and my family. That is when I remembered a specific scene from the iconic Hollywood blockbuster, *The Matrix,* which was released in 1999. This is the scene where Neo, played by Keanu Reeves, is offered a choice between a red or blue pill by Morpheus, played by Laurence Fishburne.

> This is your last chance. After this, there is no turning back. You take the blue pill, the story ends. You wake up in your bed and believe whatever you want to. You take the red pill, you stay in Wonderland, and I show you how deep the rabbit hole goes. Remember, all I'm offering is the truth. Nothing more. (*The Matrix*, 1999)

I am reminded that this quote is the perfect representation of real life. Who would have thought that a famous Hollywood movie could help us find some clarity among the broken shards of our lives? Let's break down the scene together so that we can fully grasp the life lesson. Each pill represents something different. The red pill presents you with the path of finding out the truth behind the lies. It provides you with the opportunity to change your skewed vision and change your knowledge and perception of reality. The blue pill presents you with a life of ignorance. It offers no real value to your life other than to protect you from pain and the possibility of shattering the bubble you have cocooned yourself in.

We are all given a choice in life. There are no right or wrong choices, but you do have to realize that all choices have more choices. Therefore, it is important to choose the path you envision for your life following a traumatic experience. I chose to take the red pill. I knew that I needed to accept the new normal in my life. The loss of a loved one, Dad, has shown me how delicate life is. While we as humans may be fragile, we can grow stronger after a tragedy. Once we have taken that red pill, there is no going back. Reality tells us that we cannot undo what has been done. Reality is gently nudging us to move forward until the next life event. But, as we slowly adapt to the new normal, we also accept that life is about making memories regardless of whether they are good or bad. The red pill, friends, is the new normal we are faced with after the death of a loved one.

Support and Guidance: Baby Steps

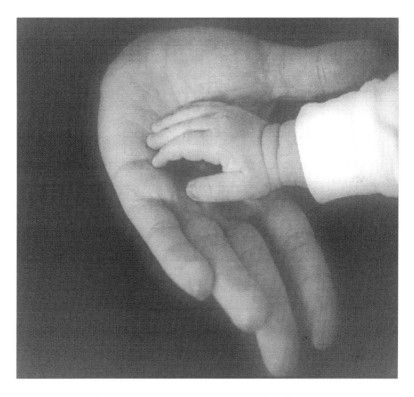

You might be experiencing a rush of adrenaline coursing through your veins or you may be feeling paralyzed and unable to move. Take a moment to take a deep breath and let it all sink in. Your world has been flipped upside down and if you want to help your family, you need to take stock of the events that have unfolded.

Your loved ones may have had the time to prepare a list of what they wanted to happen after their passing. Your heart aches thinking about your loved one being informed of their diagnosis and the probability of their life expectancy but yet you are impressed that they had the mental clarity to think about the future of those they were leaving behind. I am not saying that everyone has the same experience, especially when a seemingly healthy person is having dinner one moment and the next, they are frantically calling friends to help them because they are having a stroke. Death cannot be scheduled.

I know it is depressing to think about planning the steps to take place after your death while you are still healthy and in good shape. But, it is better to be prepared than caught with your pants around your ankles. You have the chance to plan for the sendoff of your dreams, as well as ensure that all your affairs are in order. Not everyone has that chance. Thankfully, Dad had made all the necessary decisions during the eight months after his diagnosis. All that we had to do was take care of some minor details such as contacting the doctor to pronounce Dad, calling the funeral home to come and collect him, and phone friends and family to inform them of the news. Oh, that wasn't all we had to do but those were the most important steps following Dad's passing.

Keep Calm: Support System Loading

Everyone in this world needs a support system. It doesn't matter what you are going through or experiencing during your journey. You need a support system to help congratulate you on the good days, encourage you on the bad days, cheer for you on the happy days, and cry with you on the sad days. Gillian, Stephen, and I committed to supporting Mum with whatever she wanted or needed from us. We were sure to be within earshot if she wanted to be alone or we listened to her as she talked. Honestly, we didn't know what we were doing because this was a first for all of us. Thankfully, our instincts kicked in and we were guided through the process of support and grieving.

I may not be a mind reader, nor am I an expert, but I'm pretty intuitive when it comes to assessing the feelings of my loved ones. You kind of pick up on these little tidbits in the moment. I didn't know what to do or what Mum, Gillian, or I would need. I shot up some prayers and instinct kicked in. I don't claim to be an expert on being an emotional support person, but I have to share what worked for our family.

Be Attentive

Grief has a cloak of many layers. These layers have no specific order in which they are unveiled. Most people don't even recognize the signs. It is for that reason that you should be attentive. Don't smother your parent by following them around everywhere but also don't assume all is well and head off to the pub to drown your woes in a pint of beer. This is an ideal opportunity to understand what your parent is going through.

Forgetfulness

Don't be alarmed if your parent becomes forgetful. This is one of those hidden layers I mentioned. They might confuse your names, put the sugar bowl in the fridge and the milk in the cupboard, or speak in jumbled sentences. Instead of jumping on *that* train, as I have mentioned previously, talk to your parent and calm them down. Help them by guiding them back into the present. Assure them that you are there to help them.

Short Attention Span

Concentration and forgetfulness are friends. The two together are up to no good. These two teamed up long before the loss of a loved one. Concentration is a problem on its own at the best of times, but when it is paired with grief, the effects are amplified. Don't be alarmed if your parent changes their train of thought mid-task or abruptly changes the topic of conversation. Grief will set up a maze in their minds and will have them bumping into all different types of obstacles. Be patient with your parent, and don't make them feel insecure.

Lack of Excessive Motivation

Grief can go either way where motivation comes into question. Some people clam up, curl into a ball, and refuse to do anything. They have no drive and feel that their world will never be the same because they lost the other half of their existence. On the other hand, you have people that use grief to their advantage and want to be kept busy so they either work, bake, cook, clean the house, or work in the garden. Grief doesn't come with a set of rules, and neither of these actions is cause for concern.

If your parent is showing signs of not being interested in anything and has no motivation to get out of bed, coax them out of their bubble. Be gentle with them. Allow them to grieve, and grieve with them. Share stories, ask questions, laugh, or cry. This little exercise will help both you and your parents. If you have a parent who just keeps going, be close but don't crowd them. Hover in the background because the time will come when their bubble will crack and they will begin their mourning process.

Keep Calm: Support System Loaded

You have been equipped with the tools of identifying any potential grief trigger warnings, and some guidance on how to help your grieving loved one. The time has come to divide and conquer. Your parent may not be ready to deal with the next steps, which involve tasks such as informing people of the passing, writing an obituary, writing the eulogy, or speaking at the funeral or memorial service. Dealing with the death of a parent is already difficult, but looking at all that needs to be done is downright overwhelming to the point where you may feel like running away or heading to that local pub we mentioned earlier.

Guess what? I know this may come as a shock to you, because it did to me and millions of others who have gone through it. But you don't have to be the hero, the glue, or the one that *has* to do everything. You may ask for help. It is okay not to be okay, and it is perfectly normal to ask for divine intervention. Make a list of everything that needs to be done. Get input from your family and let your parent have the final say over who does what and how it should be done. Giving them that little task of making the final decisions will be healing for them, as well as for yourself and your family.

Letting Everyone Know

This is something that requires a personal exchange. Close friends and family want to hear about the passing of your parent from you. They don't want to be reading about it on one or all of the social media platforms, nor do they want to be informed about it in the obituary column of the local newspaper. Don't try and do everything yourself, either. Share the contact lists with your siblings and others who graciously offer their assistance. It is okay to accept help.

The Obituary

There is no need for a power struggle after a parent passes away. It doesn't matter whether you are the oldest, the youngest, or if you think you are the better choice for the task. In the aftermath of losing a parent, everyone should be standing together to support each other. Allow your parent to decide who will write the obituary. For all you know, they may want to write it themselves. Your recently departed parent may have singled out someone else when they drew up their will. Don't be disappointed if you are not chosen for the task. Be supportive if someone else is going to write it or accept all the help that is offered if you are writing it.

- Share a personal story about your hero/heroine.
- It is safe to assume that all close friends and relatives have been informed of the passing, and you can share details such as time, place, and who was with them.
- Share memories of their childhood years that include where they lived, if they were academics or sports scholars, and what kind of person they were growing up.
- Mention their passion and what excited them during their lifetime.
- Talk about the love they had for their spouse.
- Share your memory that will never be erased from your mind.
- Share details such as the date, time, and place for the funeral or memorial service.

- You may mention that charitable donations to various organizations would be appreciated instead of flowers.
- End off by thanking people for support during the trying time.

The Eulogy

You, friends, and family have been asked to deliver a eulogy at the funeral or memorial service. You may have been to a service and watched how everyone stepped forward to speak about their loved one with fond memories, share some funny stories, or utter one word and break down. "I would never be able to do that" flashed through your mind. Yet, here you are and you have been asked to speak about your rock and anchor. You feel terror, your anxiety starts climbing to dangerously high levels, and the very thought has your mouth feeling like you've eaten a box of street chalk.

Stop. Take a deep breath. Inhale slowly through your nose. Hold your breath for 10 seconds. Exhale slowly through your mouth. You have got this. Public speaking is not on everybody's to-do list, but you've got this. This is your opportunity to pay tribute to your parent. They may not be there in their physical form, but believe that they are listening and hearing you in their spiritual bodies.

There are no right or wrong ways when it comes to eulogies. Many people prefer writing their thoughts down and others prefer speaking from the heart. You can borrow inspiration from the obituary if you are lost for words. This is your moment to share your memories. It is okay to laugh. It is okay to cry. You can do whatever you need to do to keep their memories fresh. You can talk about anything you want, such as:

- Memories they shared when they were younger.
- Your relationship with them.
- Their accomplishments in their career.
- Any achievements they may have gathered throughout their lifetime.
- Your favorite memories.
- Life lessons passed down.

My Story: Part 2

Mum, Gillian, Stephen, Matthew, Rosie, and I surrounded Dad's bed after he expelled his last breath at 19:26 on November 23rd, 2020. We held each other tightly and let our tears flow freely. I remember that Mum looked at me through her tears as we stood beside Dad and softly said: "Do you want his watch, Son? Dad would want that." Mum then removed Dad's watch from his wrist and put it in my hand. I looked down at his watch in my hand and had half expected it to have stopped ticking. It hit me that time goes on regardless of what happens in our lives.

I know Matthew, my nephew, collects watches. He is an amazing young man and I am proud to be his uncle. I looked at Matthew and I handed him Dad's watch. "I'd like you to have Granddad's watch. Look after it for him." He broke down in tears as he accepted the watch in thanks and sat down at the end of the bed, almost as if his legs wouldn't hold him.

The time had come for us to leave Dad's beside. It was hard to leave him there, but we had to focus and take care of some details that couldn't wait. The first item on our list was to call the doctor. They had to come out to confirm Dad's passing for legal reasons concerning the death certificate. Dad had taken care of most of the details during the eight months of his illness. He had chosen which funeral home he wanted to use. I called them and the coroner arrived approximately three hours later.

We asked the coroners to keep Dad's clothes for us, and they assured us that we could collect them from the office before his cremation. And then the inevitable happened—they took Dad away. The bed was empty. Dad had left his home where he had lived for over 40 years. He would never physically return to his home. Mum and Dad had kept the house in great shape and performed all the maintenance to keep it from falling apart. Who would take care of the maintenance now? Who would perform the necessary repairs now? There were so many questions and concerns for Mum. All these questions and concerns fall under the category of the "new normal" now.

We went to the funeral home the next day to start planning for a day and time to celebrate Dad's life with friends, family, and the community. We confirmed a date that was three weeks away. This gave us ample time to grieve and just support each other. The first day without Dad was so surreal. I found myself hearing a door creak open and almost got excited thinking that Dad was home. Almost as soon as you feel that excitement bubbling, you are doused with the freezing reality that he was no longer here. Stephen, who was the executor, read Dad's last will and testament to the immediate family. We all sat in the living room and listened as Stephen read what Dad had said. We were not listening to what was in the will, but we were listening to see what Dad's wishes were.

As Stephen read Dad's will, we all realized we had made a huge mistake. Dad had asked that his body be donated to medical science for research purposes! Dad had never mentioned this before, not to Mum, Gillian, or me, so we had no idea. I called the funeral home to tell them of this development and they advised me that I needed to call the Liverpool Hospital of Research. I called and they told me that it was too late. Because the funeral home had taken Dad's body away the previous night, they had already completed the embalming process where they injected it with formaldehyde. We were informed that the hospital could not use his body because of that. We all agreed that this was a blessing to us.

Oh, we knew that Dad would be looking down from his heavenly window seat laughing at us because we had messed up. It might not have been what Dad had initially wanted, but we knew that he would have been okay with us messing this up. This meant that we could have our funeral and cremation knowing that it was with his whole body. I remember when I left England to move to the United States. Dad told me, "I'm going to think of your move as you just going away on a long vacation and that you'll be home soon." He then went on to say I was a selfish bastard. That was Dad; tough as nails but just a big ol' softy. Yes, I know that Dad was laughing at us.

We had three weeks before the funeral. There was so much to do. We worked together and conquered all that needed to be done, from organizing the invitation list and ordering the flowers to writing the obituary. The funeral home was awesome and they walked alongside us every step of the way. We chose Dad's coffin, the urn for his ashes, music to be played, and who would receive which keepsakes. Dad loved feeding the birds in the back garden, and one of the birds that visited him nearly every day was a red robin. We decided to buy red robin lapel pins for each of the immediate family in remembrance of Dad.

We got everything done over the next couple of weeks. I had Mum give me a list of chores that needed to be done. I used Dad's tools to fix the wall tiles in the kitchen, power-washed the driveway, and emptied the attic. I made sure to keep busy for the entire three weeks leading up to the funeral. One of the toughest challenges and, in my opinion, the most painful, was sorting through the accounts and utility bills. I had no idea how many nor how long that would take. There were 27 different businesses and companies that needed to be contacted. We contacted the cable provider, the car insurance, and even the social security agency. We had to remove Dad's name and make Mum the primary. I contacted life insurance companies, sent copies of Dad's death certificate to everyone, and made sure that Mum didn't have to deal with anything after I went back to the United States.

Every day I had to listen to people saying: "I'm so sorry for your loss." There were times when I wanted to tell them where to shove it, but I knew they were well-meaning. Thank goodness I got to speak to Alison and Jessica daily. I missed them during this time. I would talk to Dad during the quieter moments. I would ask Dad and God to give me the strength and wisdom that I needed to help me get over these hurdles. To this day, I still speak to both my Fathers who are in heaven. Because of my beliefs, I know that Dad is watching me and God is keeping him company (and probably having a giggle when Dad says something out of frustration). I loved you yesterday, I love you today, and I'll love you for all the tomorrows to come.

Chapter 3:

The Perfect Send-Off

The day of the funeral or memorial service arrives. You are filled with mixed emotions. Chapter 2 took you through the planning stages and what you should do and what you could expect. Funerals are emotional affairs and affect families both emotionally as well as physically. It is a reminder that you are paying your respects to your loved one. The farewell is more for the benefit of family and friends that have been dormant for years. I have opinions about those people, but I will keep them to myself for fear of Dad reaching down from his heavenly perch and cuffing me on the side of my head!

I would like you to keep in mind that, although Dad chose to have a funeral, not everyone wants one. Your loved one may not have had the foresight to express their wishes upon their passing. If that were the case, then you need to think about what they would prefer by taking their personality into account. Remember, it is not about what you want—it is about what your loved one would want.

Something else to keep in mind when the day of the funeral arrives is that it is not about "who did it best." Each funeral is unique for the person you are paying tribute to. Most funerals are planned around the person's religious upbringing. Then some people may want to keep the service light-hearted because that was the request. This chapter is an aid to help you cope with your emotions and offer support to the remaining parent. This is where you, your siblings, and your extended family surround your parent with love, support, and protection. Oh, they will fight you off and tell you that they don't need any "faffing," but secretly they are finding the comfort you are offering.

The Day Has Arrived

The day has arrived to celebrate the coming together of family and friends to participate in the perfect sendoff that your loved one could have wished for. I say that it is perfect because whatever happens on the day is going to happen the way it should. You spend hours, days, or weeks meeting with the funeral home, the church, the crematorium, the florists, the bakery, and the deli to ensure that everything will run like a well-oiled machine. Don't fret too much if the wheels come off during the planning, execution, or the actual event. Your dearly departed loved one will not judge you should this happen and, in all likelihood, they may just be pressing some buttons to let you know that you don't have to wear the armor of protection around your heart.

The Funeral or Memorial Service Help Guide

Most funeral homes will have a dedicated team that will help you plan and execute your loved one's tribute. The funeral director will take care of all the details such as arranging for the coffin to be transported to the church, arranging for the minister, transport to the crematorium after the service, showing guests to their seats, handing out funeral notices, and helping the family with whatever they need. I do believe that everyone should make provisions in their last will and testament to have the funeral home assist with all the details. My Dad was one clever man who had the foresight to know that we would need all the help possible.

What happens if you don't want someone to help plan the funeral? It's perfectly okay if you do not want the help of the funeral home. I know of many families who handled all the details themselves. There is no shame on anyone for the choices they make. If you feel as if people don't approve of the service of choice, make sure to make eye contact and glance at the door. Chances are, they will look down at the notice in their hands and try to make themselves very small because of embarrassment. A funeral is not meant to be a circus or a costume party; a funeral is an awards ceremony where you get to pay tribute to your loved one.

Let's take a look at some of the roles that funeral directors perform to assist families. My list includes but is not limited to an array of different tasks.

- They will escort mourners into the church.
- They will ensure that the flowers are strategically placed around the pulpit, along the pews, or on the coffin.
- They will make sure that the right body was sent (accidents do occur).
- They will ensure that the family does not incur late fees for mourners who do not leave after the service.
- They will provide pallbearers to carry the coffin if the family has not chosen their own.
- They offer the service of having the wake at the venue of the service.

Again, you get to choose whether you need or want the help of a funeral director. Don't worry about offending them if you decide to decline their services because they still offer support behind the scenes such as ensuring that the coffin gets to the church, possible body switches, and the funeral notices.

Before the Funeral

The morning of the service approaches faster than you anticipated. Your first thoughts when opening your eyes are that of disbelief. You want to bury your head in the pillow and burrow under the covers. This is the day when you have to cloak yourself in the strongest armor you can find to protect you from falling apart. You reluctantly roll out of bed and stop to look at yourself in the mirror. You want to have a stern word with yourself, but words fail as the tear taps are opened.

Of course, by now you know that everyone will have a different experience on the day of their loved one's funeral service. Yes, it is going to be a day filled with so many different emotions. These are emotions you might anticipate but yet have no control over what happens. I can share with you that you will want to sleep for a couple of days. You will feel a type of exhaustion that you have never experienced, as well as a sense of relief that it is over. Then again, you will start feeling all types of other feelings at having to return to your life. Let's take a look at what you could be doing before you leave for the church.

- Have a good, wholesome breakfast.
- Stay hydrated.
- Rehearse the eulogy.
- Take a brisk walk to keep the nerves intact.
- Pack a snack bag and bottled water for your parent to keep the energy levels up.
- Pack a little first aid kit with necessities such as tissues, eye drops, lip balm, and a toothbrush.
- Take in your surroundings and remember all the details.
- It's okay to cry.

There are many different tips and tricks you can do to make this day easier for your parent and family members. I will be speaking about signs in an upcoming chapter. These signs could be anything that might be an indication that your loved one is with you. Many signs surround us such as something visual, something to do with your senses, or just a general gut feeling that your loved one is with you. You will get through the day. Everything will be okay.

At the Church

You and your family arrive at the church before the guests. The funeral director (if you choose to have one) and the minister or priest are at the church to greet you. They usher you into a side room and take you through the timeline of how the service will go. Depending on your religion or preferences, your minister can pray with your family for strength and comfort, as well as participate in a familial communion.

You will be shown where you will be seated for the service. Immediate family members such as parents, spouses, children, children's spouses/partners, and grandchildren of the dearly departed loved one will be seated in the first few pews. You may have made arrangements with your siblings about who would be greeting guests as they enter the church, at which point you make your way to the entrance. Remember now, you will most likely be seeing people you last saw when you were knee-high or people you have never met before but have heard much about. You may just want to bite down on your tongue when they enter the church all weepy, you know—your loved one, heavenly perch, cuff to the side of the head...

Let's take a look at how a typical funeral service will look. Just a reminder that there are many different types of religions and religious denominations, so funeral services will look different for everyone. Also, because we are living in uncertain times with a certain global pandemic that mutates as the season changes, funeral services will look different, and in-person attendance might not be possible. Most funeral services offer Zoom meetings where friends and family that cannot be there in person can watch from the comfort of their homes.

- Arrive at the church approximately an hour before the service begins.
- Meet with the minister and the funeral director.
- See where you will be seated.

- Greet guests at the entrance of the church.
- Opening prayer.
- Scripture reading.
- Sing a song.
- Share the eulogy.
- Prayer.
- A short sermon.
- A couple of appreciation messages to everyone who helped you through the process.
- An invitation to the after-funeral gathering.

You don't have to nor are you expected to be strong and keep your emotions hidden. There is no shame whatsoever if you cry or laugh at the funeral service of your loved one. I have heard from someone who said that people at the service thought the eldest daughter was on drugs because she showed no emotions and instead looked around behind her to see who had come to honor her loved one. In truth, the daughter had spent nine weeks before the death showing her love and crying when no one was around. On the day of the death, the daughter was the one who was there and even though the passing was instant, she held it together for her grandmother and younger sister. The daughter still mourns the loss but it is not a sad mourning, it is a mourning of remembrance and looking for signs that her loved one is around her through the good, the bad, the fun, and the sad days. (Keep reading for the chapter about signs.)

After the Funeral Service

Most people have a reception after the service where everyone can enjoy a cup of tea, some snacks, and a catch-up to remember the loved one you have just paid tribute to. These receptions can take place at the church, the funeral home, a local restaurant/pub, or at the home of the loved one. Some people prefer to have a private reception to celebrate their loved ones and save on costs, and others may like to include all guests to have a meet and greet. Especially those that have hidden in the woodwork your entire life and have suddenly surfaced. Note to self: Lock doors and keep a close eye on all guests! Oh, I'm just joking—sort of—*ouch,* Dad!

You don't have to feel obligated or forced into a corner to have a reception. The whole idea of having an after-funeral gathering is to share stories and remember your loved one. It is not about the type of food, the quantity, or the beverages being served. It is not a party but a voluntary gesture from a grieving family that wants to give others the chance to share their memories. Let's take a look at some helpful tips for organizing an after-funeral reception at the family home.

- Ask for and accept help.
- Make lists of what needs to be done.
- Delegate chores such as cleaning the house, washing bowls, plates, cups, glasses, and polishing the silverware.
- Set out photos and trinkets that represent your loved one.
- Decide whether you want to have a sit-down dinner or if you will have platters of snacks.
- Don't be a hero and turn down help.
- You don't have to serve alcohol at the reception.

There are hundreds of different ways to celebrate your loved one after the funeral service. Receptions fall under the personal choice category, and you should do what you feel is appropriate. You could even restrict the guest list to include those who formed part of your immediate family. Instead of having a reception where people come to eat, drink, and remember, you could plant a tree or have a park bench dedicated in honor of your loved one, as Gillian did for Dad. There are so many different ways to celebrate your loved one, and all it takes is a little bit of imagination and creativity.

My Story: Part 3

Alison managed to join me in England a week before the funeral service. We weren't sure she would make it because of all the pandemic rules and regulations. I held my breath, because no one seemed to know what was happening from one moment to the next. Alison let me know that she would be coming, and oh boy, did I need her. You see, Alison is my strength and inspiration.

Mum, Stephen, Gillian, Matthew, and Rosie all decided that I would read the eulogy at Dad's funeral. I graciously accepted, but only if Gillian stood up there with me. We all sat down together and discussed what we would say in the eulogy. It started with Dad's youth, his schooling, and achievements, his first job, and when and how he met Mum. We spoke about how much he cared for, protected, and loved Mum and us. The final result was a masterpiece that represented something special for each of us. We all had the chance to add a special moment with Dad that we wanted to share. We included Stephen, Mathew, Rosie, Alison, and Jessica in the sharing of memories part of the eulogy. I finished the eulogy with a summary and then ended it off with a funny joke. How could I not include something funny? Dad enjoyed seeing happy people.

The funeral home let us know that Dad was in his coffin at their location. They told us that we could visit him if we wanted to. Mum, Gillian, Alison, and I went to the funeral home. This was the first time since Dad had passed away that we were going to see him. We each had the opportunity to view Dad on our own. I braced myself when my turn came around. I honestly didn't know what to expect when I looked into the coffin. Dad looked like Dad. He had color in his cheeks and it honestly looked as if he was sleeping. I was almost afraid to make any noise for fear of waking him up. I reached out and held his hand. I talked to Dad and told him how sorry I was for making mistakes in my life. I apologized for giving him a hard time while growing up. I thanked him for his patience, understanding, support, and love. I told him how much I would miss him. I gave him permission, although he didn't need it, to visit, talk, and let me know when he felt I needed a shove in the right direction or that cuff on the ear if he felt I was being a jerk. I finally told him that we would be together again one day and that he should keep my seat warm.

We visited Dad several times that week, getting in as many last-minute visits before the day of the funeral service. Before one of our visits, we had all decided to write a letter to Dad. Each letter was personal and private from us to him. No one else would read those letters. We wrote down things we wanted to say that we may never have had the opportunity to say when Dad was with us. We put the letters in envelopes, and the day before the service, I went to see Dad for the final time. I gave him kisses from each of us—the final kiss I gave him was from Mum. I reassured him how much we loved him and how much we missed him. I also told him that we would all be okay. I placed the envelopes in the coffin, by his side, to be cremated with him the next day.

I spent the night before the funeral rehearsing the eulogy several times. I had it memorized, but fear snuck in and toyed with me, making me believe that I would somehow mess up. In short, I exhausted myself to the point where I couldn't think straight anymore. I woke up the morning of the funeral feeling energized and without any of the self-doubts I had the night before. We had breakfast, had a casual conversation about the usual things, and included Dad in our banter. Yes, it was going to be a good day—a sad one but a good one.

The Day of Dad's Funeral Service

Gillian and I walked down to the local florist around 10 a.m. to pick up the white roses we had pre-ordered. There were roses from all of us, including our belated brother, Andrew, may he R.I.P. The day before the funeral service, I had bought a small bottle of Johnnie Walker Scotch, Red Label. This specific drink was one of Winston Churchill's favorite drinks. I thought that if I was going to have a toast to Dad, that this would be all the more special. I think I drank most of the bottle before the funeral, but strangely enough, I didn't feel a thing. It was odd because I felt fine. I was calm and at peace with the day. I do remember Mum asking if I was okay, and yes, I was okay, because I had never felt stronger.

Some of the family and friends started to arrive at the house shortly after lunch. Most waited outside in their cars. I was ready. I chose to wear one of Dad's old white shirts, an old work suit, and his old black shoes. Dad was definitely with us that day. The hearse and limousines arrived shortly after 1 p.m. The funeral conductor came into the house to speak to the immediate family. She was dressed in a black tail and waistcoat with black pants, a black top hat, and a black and silver cane. It was like it was in the 1860s. I was impressed, and yet it was so surreal.

She calmed us and told us not to worry about anything. We were reminded that the most important thing for us to do as a family was to take our time and that things would fall into place. When we were ready, Gillian, Stephen, Matthew, Rosie, Alison, myself, and Mum walked out of the house. Family and friends had created a path from the house to the hearse where Dad was waiting for us. There was not a sound as we made the walk down the path to the hearse. The silence that filled the air was deafening. It was the darkest moment of my life. I took a deep breath and stepped forward. One by one, we placed our white roses on Dad's coffin. We turned and walked towards the limousines behind Dad's hearse. As I glanced back, I noticed that each time the conductor walked past Dad's coffin, she would stop, remove her hat, and tip her head towards Dad as a sign of respect. I knew that he would have liked that.

The church was only a 10-minute walk from the house. We could have walked, but the conductor told us that we would be driving the long way around so that Dad could wave goodbye to his town. I watched again as the conductor took her place in front of the hearse and started slowly walking down the road as the hearse and limousines drove behind. There was a rather large crowd of people waiting outside the church as we pulled up. A glance around the crowd showed old neighbors, friends, and Dad's old co-workers from years gone by. I know, for sure, that Dad was smiling with pride at how many people had shown up to say their farewells and show their support for Mum and the family.

We stood outside the church for a moment and greeted as many people as we could before the pallbearers were called over. I was one of the pallbearers. They gave us instructions on how to gather the coffin from the hearse, raise it to our shoulders, and carry Dad into the church. Carrying Dad is a weight I will never forget. He was a tall and slim man. Maybe the weight came from the coffin. Maybe I was the only one feeling weight. I will be honest and tell you that I'll never forget how heavy Dad felt to me. I can also tell you, without any shadow of a doubt, that I do not care how heavy Dad was in his coffin. I would willingly and lovingly walk a thousand miles carrying him on my shoulders if the chance ever presented itself.

The Final Goodbye

The church service was perfect. We could not have asked for anything more fitting. The priest, who knew our family very well, spoke very eloquently about Dad. It was a spiritual, funny, down-to-earth, and very emotional service. At the end of the service, we picked up Dad, carried him back to the hearse, and drove to the crematorium. We had an entourage waiting for us when we arrived at the crematorium. A group of family and friends who had not gone to the church had met us at the crematorium. It was amazing.

The service at the crematorium was very short and only lasted 30 minutes. This was because of the global pandemic and the restrictions that had been put in place. We walked into the crematorium carrying Dad for the final time. We were greeted by a song playing on the speakers which was "Z Cars" for

Everton Football Club. This song was for a rival team to the team that Dad supported. If you didn't know, Dad was a Liverpool supporter. Dad chose the song himself because Gillian and her family were Everton supporters!

We placed Dad at the front of the congregation and took our seats. The priest from our church, Father Pat, spoke for a few minutes to give me enough time to deliver the eulogy. Before I could proceed with the eulogy, it was time for Dad's second song, "*Who Wants to Live Forever*" by Queen. I'd heard the song many times before, but hearing it again at Dad's funeral made me listen to the words. That's a tough song to listen to. My sister and I took to the podium. I pulled out my eulogy notes, a few reminders to help guide me. There was a microphone and a speaker system to help project my voice. I wanted everyone to hear what I had to say.

I spoke for 20 minutes. I felt that I made Dad proud and that my family and I did a good job of piecing everything together. I did manage to get through all my talking points, and yes, I did get choked up once or twice—okay, several times. There were moments when I had to take a deep breath to calm my nerves. Having my sister at my side helped me stay calm enough to proceed. At the end of the eulogy, Dad's third song played. It was the Liverpool Football Club's stadium anthem, "*You'll Never Walk Alone*" by Gerry and the Pacemakers. Truth be told, that was an even harder song to listen to, and I don't think I'll ever be able to listen to it without crying.

The New Normal Commences

Gillian, Stephen, Matthew, Rosie, Alison, and I walked out of the crematorium first. I got to the rear exit and looked back to see Mum standing at Dad's coffin. She was crying her heart out while touching the brass nameplate. We gathered around outside for a few minutes before the next funeral arrived. We hugged family and friends and said our goodbyes before settling into the limousines for the final drive home—without Dad.

When we got home and walked in through the door, it hit me. Everything around me was Dad. The whole house was filled with his memories. It was his things and possessions. It was his handyman work. His car. His toolshed. His seat at the dining table. His armchair in the living room. Everything in the house had been touched by him. Dad was all around me.

It was as if he was still here but not physically in the room. It was as if he was in another room or upstairs. I kept expecting him to walk in and everything would be okay again. I felt that he wasn't far away. It was the strangest feeling. I love you, Dad.

Chapter 4:

Life Goes On: Putting the Pieces Back Together

The death of a loved one is something that rocks the foundation that your life is built on. Your world slows down when your loved one is first diagnosed with an incurable disease. You don't want to think about it, yet it is in your face. You finally make peace with the news and your world returns to a new normal. Just as you are making peace with the diagnosis, your loved one passes away. Your world doesn't slow down; it comes to a complete stop. The rocky foundation of your life has crumbled to dust.

Friends, family, and acquaintances offer support and comfort. You have a choice of accepting or rejecting the offers to help you through your grieving process. I have mentioned multiple times that each person experiences and deals with grief in their way. There are no right or wrong ways to grieve. You cannot put a time to grieve on your desktop calendar. Grief is a natural process that everyone has to go through. Don't listen to the person who tells you that "you'll get over it." That little phrase is even worse than hearing someone tell you that "they are in a better place."

Maybe your loved one is in a better place and you will get over it—eventually. These are not statements you want to hear when you are in the beginning stages of grief. In all honesty, you are still trying to wrap your head around the fact that your loved one won't be on the other end of the phone or video when you call them. The truth is, from one grieving son to other grievers, it is scary to think about picking up the pieces and moving forward when all you want is to step back in time to make different choices.

Honestly, there is no time limit on when or if you will ever feel "normal" after the loss of a loved one. Putting those pieces together again is going to be a moment by moment, day by day, week by week, month by month, and year by year process. Don't rush the process, and take as long as you need. Don't ever let anyone tell you that you "should get over it," because there is no such thing.

Peeling Back the Layers of the Cloak of Grief

I have touched on the cloak of grief and its many layers in previous chapters. I have given a couple of hints at what some of the layers could look like. I have even given a couple of warnings that not everyone will experience the effects that are found beneath the layers of the grief cloak. Grief doesn't warn you when it is about to possess you, and some people may experience the layers during and straight after the grieving process. Others may experience the layers of grief for years. Some may need the help of medical professionals and medication to deal with the effects of grief.

This cloak of grief is not here to destroy your life. Nothing can do that unless you give it power over you. Grief is not a shame-worthy condition, and no one should be made to feel guilty or hide the fact that they are grieving. Not everyone grieves the same way, nor do they follow the same patterns. I want to take you on a little trip around the cloak of grief. It is not my intention to drag you down any dark passageways, nor will I tell you what you are or should be feeling at any given time. I want to share my experience, as well as those of others I have met on this journey while researching my book.

The Stages of Grief

A Swiss psychiatrist by the name of Elizabeth Kübler-Ross developed a grief model in 1969, the Kübler-Ross Grief Cycle. This model was introduced to the world in her book titled *On*

Death and Dying. The model shows that there are five stages of grief. Kübler-Ross received a fair amount of criticism for her grief model because the general population and other medical professionals were under the impression that the stages of grief happened in the order which she portrayed.

I have to give Kübler-Ross credit for identifying the stages of grief so that we have a name to attach to our feelings. I would just like to mention again that not everyone goes through the five stages of grief and not everyone will go through any of the stages. There is nothing wrong with you if you don't experience one of the five stages of grief (Gregory, 2016). Let's take a look at the them, in no particular order.

Denial

Denial is a vital part of the stages of grief. Your first instinct is that of disbelief when you find out about a loved one's health diagnosis or the passing of a loved one. You know it is true because no one should lie about health or death, but your mind shuts down and you don't want to process the news you have been given. You don't want to believe the news and you want to be the hero to prove that everyone else has made a terrible mistake. All you are doing is suppressing your feelings and the truth. Your shock receptors are the guiding force of your denial. Shock and denial will join hands as they begin to fade away. Their departure will leave behind a key unlocking the feelings you had locked away. Don't be afraid to unlock your feelings. You want to open up that door and you want to feel everything. That is when your healing will begin. In truth, there is nothing better than a good old ugly cry session to heal you from the inside out.

Bargaining

It is part of our human nature to bargain our way out of situations. Who do you turn to when you want to bargain with something that is beyond human control? Of course, you turn to your religious beliefs. I believe in God, but there is no judgment for anyone who you turn to for some supernatural assistance. You spend hours on your knees praying, begging, and pleading for your deity to reverse the outcome. People will become desperate because they believe that their requests are not being heard or answered. You are faced with the worst-case scenario—your loved one passes on and you are left with anger.

Anger

Yes, this part of grief is not a very pleasant little layer on the cloak. Anger alone can lead people down very dark passageways. Many don't come back from those experiences because they blame everyone and their religion for everything that goes wrong. They lose their faith because they are enveloped in a layer of anger and hatred. Can you emerge from that layer and find your light again? Absolutely! That is one of the most beautiful aspects of religion. God doesn't turn His back on us—we turn our backs on Him. Expect that you will be angry, but don't go down any dark passageways because I can guarantee that you will be lonelier than you have ever been. This is something I have heard from other grieving friends that found their way back before they burned bridges.

Depression

Depression is a disorder you do not want to ignore. It affects your mood and unknowingly affects the way you see the world around you. You may feel a deep sadness and you might have no interest in participating in your usual activities. Grief is not something that comes with a switch, and you cannot know from one moment to the next how you will be feeling. Don't hide your feelings in the layers of your grief cloak. If you suspect that you may be suffering from depression stemming from the death of a loved one, please see your medical professional.

Depression is that dark passageway I have been describing in previous sections. Those passageways are the ones you want to avoid getting stuck in because they are scary places. I have heard from various people that it could take anywhere from days to years to find the light. Grief related to illness or health is a major trigger for depression, but there are many other factors that contribute such as family history or genetics, addiction to alcohol, medication or street drugs, and personality (Bruce, 2021).

Acceptance

This is when you realize that life goes on. Your loved one is not with you in the physical form, but they will live on in your heart and memories for all eternity. This is the last step of the grieving process according to the Kübler-Ross Grief Cycle. Grief doesn't follow any rules or protocols, as mentioned at the beginning of this section. You can slide through multiple stages of grief multiple times at any given time. I do want to reassure you that you are allowed to smile and be happy. Do you know why it is okay? Because if you are happy, your loved one is proudly smiling down on you knowing that the healing has started. You are no longer pining for them because you have realized that your life has to continue. You have a destiny to fulfill. Your loved one lived their life and they conquered the dragon that needed to be slain. It is your chance now.

Coping Strategies

Grief has a way of sticking around and striking when you least expect it. You can be fine one moment, and the next you may be filled with a sense of intense sadness and an ache that comes from deep inside your soul. You start looking around for what caused this sudden change in your emotions. A glance at the calendar, for instance, will send shockwaves through your body as you remember something significant you and your loved one did. This is known as a trigger, and, spoiler alert, there are *many* such triggers which I am going to drag you along to look at with me.

I am sharing these triggers with you not to make you sad but to show you that you don't have to be afraid. We have all been down this little path many times, and it is perfectly normal to experience the grief that is associated with these triggers. It is how you cope with these triggers that will make the difference. You don't have to avoid special holidays, occasions, or moments because you are afraid you may have a meltdown. Cry if you want, laugh if you want, set a spot at the dinner table, or pour two drinks and enjoy them both. Don't bottle your feelings, and don't stop being yourself.

Recognizing Emotional Triggers

The loss of a loved one is something that will remain with you for the rest of your life. We know that grief is attached to our emotions. You either wear your heart on your sleeve or you lock it behind layers of concrete and steel. It doesn't matter which one you are because when it comes to emotions, they find a way to seep out and make their presence known. Emotions that are connected to grief include:

- Anxiety
- Crying
- Anger
- Loneliness
- No motivation
- Guilt
- Longing

What Could Activate Grief Triggers?

Grief triggers are as unpredictable as the weather. You never know from one moment to the next how you will feel. You may be laughing and happy one moment and the next you are a mess and gasping for air because something reminded you of your loved one. No one experiences the same emotions or triggers. Let's take a look at some of the types of triggers that could stir up emotions. Remember now, these are only examples, so don't go thinking that you are heartless because you haven't experienced any of these triggers.

- Holidays
- Anniversaries

- Birthdays
- Favorite songs
- Favorite movies
- Wedding invitations
- Birthday milestones
- Graduations
- Father/Mother wedding dance
- Favorite food
- Favorite beverage

Preparing for Possible Grief Triggers

You may be wondering whether it is possible to be prepared for these triggers or to avoid emotions. I do believe that you can identify possible triggers as best you can. However, no amount of preparation can prevent you from experiencing the emotions from the triggers. I believe that you can't avoid emotions, and yes, they are unpredictable and can occur in the blink of an eye. All I can keep stressing is that you should not suppress your emotions. Bottled-up emotions fester and cause more harm than good. Be kind to yourself at all times—it won't cost you a dime.

- Mark important days on the calendar that remind you of your loved one.
- Identify a place you can go to when grief suddenly strikes such as the bathroom, a quiet room, or a place where you can focus on something that will distract you.
- Upliftment by way of positive affirmations.
- Being prepared and anticipating a time frame that is significant to your loved one will help minimize the effect of anxiety.
- Avoid those dark passageways and always look for the light.
- Writing will help you express emotions you don't want to talk about with those around you.

This list is not meant to be one-size-fits-all but is a guide to show you possibilities of how you can prepare and deal with triggers and emotions. Create coping skills that will help you. No one knows you better than you know yourself.

My Story: Part 4

There isn't a single day that has gone by that I haven't thought about Dad. I've shed many tears in the days, weeks, and months since Dad's passing. Dad helped me get my first job, he gave me advice when I met my first girlfriend, and he helped me through every emotional and physical stage of my life. I may not always get signs or grief triggers when I want them. I have realized that they don't just appear out of thin air. I have found that on the days when I need confirmation that Dad is with me, all I need to do is think about him. Thinking about him fills me with the strength I need to get through a particularly difficult day. I believe, with every fiber of my being, that Dad is still helping me through the difficulties I am facing.

In 2020, along with millions of people across the globe, I lost my job due to the invasion of COVID-19. The insurance company I spent 15 years working at retrenched most of my department. I put in many hours and invested money into the company. I sacrificed so much. I gave them 15 years of my life, only for it all to be flushed down the tubes. I was in shock when I received the news. The shock turned to anger very quickly.

I called Dad and we discussed the situation I suddenly found myself in. Dad always had a way of making me see the silver lining around the dark clouds. He told me to see this experience as a new beginning. He further went on to tell me that it was the company's loss and that I would be better off without them. He was right, Dad always was right. I looked around for other insurance work, even though I wanted to walk away from it. I had so many bad and sad days. I pretty much felt lonely and pathetic most of the time.

I had to put on a brave face for Alison, who still had her job. At this stage, because of COVID-19, Alison was working remotely. Dad kept me going. He was such a strong man and always said the right things at the right time. Dad would encourage me to stand up and get it done. It didn't matter what it was, as long as I addressed whatever needed to be done. I'll never forget something Dad said to me: "Son, don't be worrying about the past or even the present when the future is more important."

Since Dad's passing, I've had several signs and grief triggers. I have found white feathers in places that do not make sense. I've had dreams that feel so real that when I wake up, I half expect it to carry on in real time. The dreams are so vivid and clear that I don't want to wake up. Some of the dreams show Dad in his youth. I've also had a heart-stopping moment when I heard a voice late one night: "What are you doing?" I looked around for the source of the voice. Was it Dad? I could not tell if it was his voice, but I do know that it was a man's voice. Who else could it have been?

For me, Dad is still here. He is encouraging me to carry on. I know he wants me to be happy. On the days when I am feeling lonely and down in the dumps, I can feel Dad's presence. It's his love and faith in me that keeps me going during those slumpy days. Dad's love lifts me, keeps me calm, and helps me cope with my cloak of grief that can weigh so heavy on my shoulders.

Chapter 5:

Understanding the Effects of

Grief and Stress

Chapter 4 saw you picking up the pieces of your life after the death of a loved one. You were taken on a little trip where you were introduced to the cloak of grief and its many layers. You learned about triggers, memories, and the five stages of grief. You also learned that your grief cannot be measured against anyone else's experience. You know that the various stages of grief do not come with a manual, specific guidelines, or timelines. Grief comes and goes without fanfare. It doesn't knock at the door to announce itself. Grief can arrive when you least expect it and it can leave as suddenly. The most important thing you can do for yourself is not to wait around for grief to come to you. You need to live the life you were destined for. Don't let your world stop while you wait for grief to come knocking.

- Has someone close to you been diagnosed with an illness or a disease?
- Are you mourning the loss of a loved one or friend?
- Are you going through a divorce?
- Are you in a relationship where you are being either physically and/or mentally abused?

- Have you been dismissed from your place of work?

If you have answered yes to any of the questions above, then this chapter is dedicated to you. The cloak of grief is a deceptive garment that attaches itself to anything. You may not believe you are grieving and that you "have everything under control," but I want to urge you to continue reading this chapter. You may or may not see something that triggers one or all of the layers of your cloak. I want to help you, not break you down or deceive you. I am going to share what worked for me when Dad was diagnosed when he passed away, and the days, weeks, and months after his death.

The Negative Implications of Grief and Stress

Grief on its own is difficult to deal with, but when you add stress to the mix, you are left with a lethal Molotov cocktail that can destroy you. Traumatic life experiences affect people in different ways. Not everyone will have the same experiences. Some may fare better than others and hide their grief exceptionally well. Others may wear their grief on their sleeves for all to see. There is no contest when it comes to determining who wore the cloak of grief better.

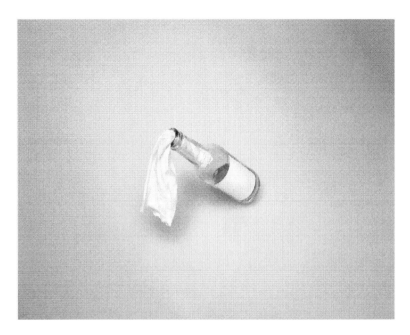

I would like to take you on another one of my detours. I hope that I can give you a better understanding of what grief and stress can do to your mind, body, and soul. I want to show you why it is important to work through your pain instead of hiding it away. I don't want anyone to end up in that dark passage, and I especially don't want you wandering around there for too long. This book and everything that is being discussed is for those of us who have something in common—the loss of someone or something that meant the world to us. We are left behind for a reason. We do not know what those reasons are. We may never know what those reasons will be. Our loved ones would not want us to wither away because of them. They definitely would not want us disconnecting from the loved ones that are still with us. They would want us to go out and be socially active, to laugh, and have fun. It's okay to live.

Symptoms of Grief

If you have experienced grief, then you will know that it can affect your ability to function normally. Catherine Burnette, Ph.D. specializes in mental health at the School of Social Work at Tulane University and has said that grief is individual and no one ever knows when or why it comes to the surface. It does make sense and drives home what has been mentioned multiple times thus far. Another example that is given is thinking about people who are angry and frustrated. You don't know that you are going to be angry in the next 10 minutes because there are no warning bells.

Let's join Catherine as she gives us a list of psychological and physical symptoms our body faces when struggling with grief. Please remember that the lists are merely a guide and not a diagnostic tool.

Psychological Symptoms

- Cannot focus or concentrate
- Irritable for no reason
- Sadness
- Feeling numb
- Anger
- Confusion

Physical Symptoms

- Constant headaches
- Unexplainable exhaustion

- Insomnia
- Loss of appetite
- Lowered immune system and picking up all types of viruses (Burnette, n.d.)

Looking at the list of symptoms gives you a glimpse of what is possible when you are dealing with grief. According to Heather Stang, an author and a grief expert with a master's degree in thanatology, our bodies do suffer when we are grieving the loss of our loved ones. Burnette's list could be expanded on to add feedback from the people who are counseled by Stang to show the severity of symptoms displayed in grieving people. The list includes:

- Tightness in the chest, muscles, and throat
- Unexplained joint pain
- Shortness of breath
- Weak muscles
- Nausea
- Dry mouth
- The sense of being clumsy all the time (Stang, n.d.)

A group of scientists from the University of St. George's London believed that the impact of grief can be detrimental to the health of people. The scientists found that the physiological responses to serious grief could lead to heart attacks or strokes (Carey et al., 2014). Maybe the line "died of a broken heart" was not just said to romanticize the situation.

Coping Tools to Treat Grief and Stress

How many times have you heard someone say "snap out of it" or "you'll get over it"? I would like to believe that the people who say these things don't know how to offer help and support after the loss of a loved one. But then... you get the people who have no filters and no feelings of sympathy because they may not have gone through a traumatic life experience. They think they are helping you by being upbeat and trying to lift your spirits, but you are not feeling it just yet. I get that you don't want to burden friends and family with your problems, because I've been there and I have met many who have and are still there.

- How do you treat the symptoms of grief you are experiencing?
- How long before these symptoms go away?
- Will they ever go away?
- Are there any magic pills and potions to make everything better?

I honestly wish I had all the answers. I reached out to others I spoke to during this journey and no one has any clarity as to when you will feel "normal" again. This is a wave you will need to ride until the waves have run their course. Please don't be discouraged because these waves are necessary to help ease you back into your new normal. Don't rush the grieving process, and take as long as you need to find your way back. I am going to share a couple of helpful activities that should help you alleviate some of the mental and physical symptoms you are experiencing.

Exercise

Now, no one is going to expect you to go to a gym, but there are many different types of exercises you can participate in within the comfort of your home, such as dancing, cleaning the house (sweeping, mopping, or vacuum cleaning), or gardening.

Gratitude List

Start each day with a list of things you are grateful for. I know things are looking a little bleak and you don't feel as if you have anything to be grateful for, but you have so much going for you. You wake up in the morning. You are breathing. You have a bed to sleep in. You have a roof over your head. You can feel the wind on your face. Start with one thing you are grateful for and build yourself up. You will soon be waking up with a smile on your face and thinking about how to limit your gratitude list.

Meditation

Take some time out to meditate when you feel that the tsunami tidal wave is threatening to overwhelm you. You can download apps on your mobile phones, find a video clip on YouTube, read from your favorite book, read and pray from the bible, or spend quiet time reflecting. Everyone needs to do what they feel most comfortable doing.

Let's take a look at some additional activities to help you during your readjustment to your new normal:

- Distract yourself by organizing an area in your home, office, or car.
- Practice breathing by inhaling through the nose, holding your breath, and exhaling through your mouth.
- Write for healing—journaling or letter writing.
- Remove yourself from an area that makes you feel caged in.
- Watch something on any of your preferred social media platforms to distract you—feel-good animal clips are almost guaranteed to put a smile on your face.
- Fill your living space with scents from candles or diffusers.
- It is important to get sufficient sleep.

Diet Change During Stressful Times

You have been equipped with the knowledge to identify the symptoms of stress and grief, and you were given a toolkit full of examples of coping with your new normal. You are probably rolling your eyes and getting ready to skip forward to the next chapter after seeing the title of this section. I don't want you thinking that I am going to tell you that you could stand to lose a couple of pounds because this book is actually about how you can lose 50 pounds in 10 days if you follow my foolproof steps. Sorry to the critics who are smiling gleefully because they knew there was more to this book. I am extremely happy to tell you that I am not going to tell you what to do, and no, this book is most definitely not some diet or lifestyle changing manual.

Remember, I am the one who is sharing my life and experiences following the death of my dad with you. I know what grief is. I have lived it. I am still living it. I have heard from many people how they are trying to keep their heads above the water because of stress and grief. I don't have any hidden agendas other than the honesty I have been sharing. Remember, Dad is sitting on his heavenly perch, and I really don't want him to cuff my ear.

Understanding Cortisol

Dieticians have revealed that certain food types have been linked to the reduction of cortisol levels. What is cortisol? I'm so happy that you asked! Cortisol is a stress hormone that is produced by the adrenal gland which is found on our kidneys and is released into our bloodstream during periods of stressful situations. In short, cortisol gives your body the energy that is needed to help cope with short-term situations. The long-term production of cortisol can negatively impact your overall health. Let's take a look at what cortisol means for you and your body.

- It helps to manage your sleep cycles.
- It helps to minimize inflammation brought on by physical stress.
- It increases your blood sugar.
- It helps your body distribute the carbs, fats, and proteins you consume.
- It helps to control your blood pressure.

Stress-Relieving Food Versus Comfort Food

I've been in the company of people where I've heard the wives of colleagues, family, or strangers talk about "eating their emotions." I guess it is the same as someone drinking alcohol to numb their pain, only to wake up the next morning and discover that the pain is still there plus they have acquired a massive headache. Let's agree to disagree that whatever you are going to do to numb the pain, whether it is eating, drinking, smoking, or whatever it is to "help" you through this difficult time in your life; it is going to end up being an expensive affair that will become a habit. I don't know if you realize it, but habits are pretty difficult to shake. I do believe that this is the first and last motivational preach I will be issuing!

Dietician Courtney Barth recommends that people who are struggling with stressful situations, which include grief, should consume an anti-inflammatory diet. Let's take a look at the types of food you should be eating to help regulate your cortisol levels.

Vitamin B

Food high in B vitamins will assist the body with regulating cortisol levels.

- Beef
- Eggs
- Organ meats such as liver, or kidneys
- Chicken
- Fortified cereal
- Nutritional yeast

Omega-3 Fatty Acid

Food in this category helps to lower inflammation.

- Anchovies
- Salmon
- Sardines
- Mackerel
- Herring
- Oysters
- Tuna
- Avocados
- Olive oil
- Walnuts
- Flax seeds
- Chia seeds

Magnesium-Rich

Food high in magnesium not only reduces inflammation and regulates cortisol levels, but it is also beneficial in aiding with the relaxation of the mind and body.

- Dark chocolate
- Pumpkin seeds
- Avocados
- Broccoli
- Bananas

Protein-Rich

A diet consisting of protein-rich food helps to balance blood sugar levels.

- Chicken breasts
- Turkey breasts
- Eggs
- Beef
- Shrimp
- Tuna
- Salmon
- Almonds
- Peanuts
- Quinoa
- Lentils

Gut-Healthy

Our guts are like Petri dishes. What we put into our bodies has to be broken down by enzymes, and then the sorting begins. I like to think that the food we consume is on parade to our organs and a selection process takes place to see who gets vitamin B or who gets the protein and then a debate about who gets to add to the love handles or muffin tops. A healthy gut will be a happy gut. The food in this category is filled with probiotics that help to keep our immune systems happy and maintain a healthy balance for our blood sugar and reduce cholesterol.

- Greek or natural yogurt
- Kefir
- Sauerkraut
- Kombucha
- Kimchi

What Should You Avoid Consuming?

No one is going to tell you what you can and cannot eat. I used to hear ladies talk about whatever diet they were on and the words "in moderation" came up quite frequently. If you don't want to give up on your favorites, why not downsize to a smaller portion and aim to have it once a week, then every two weeks, until you have broken the habit of inhaling a whole slab of chocolate or an extra-large meal at McDonald's? You are important. Your health is important. You will be missed if you don't take care of yourself. You don't know whose life you have touched by smiling at them or picking up an apple that fell in the grocery store.

Here is a list of some of the foods that stimulate your cortisol levels and cause unnecessary stress:

- Alcohol
- Sodas
- Caffeine
- Food high in sugar
- Cakes
- Cookies
- Pastries (Barth, 2021)

Supplements and Vitamins

Sleep, diet, and exercise is the most popular form of "medication" to combat stress. If you feel that these three tried and tested stress boosters are not sufficient and you are still feeling overwhelmed, then you should consider taking vitamins and supplements. Again, I am not a doctor or a holistic practitioner. The information listed in this section is from the American Institute of Stress.

- B Complex Vitamins
- Kava
- Ashwagandha
- L-Theanine
- Melatonin
- Rhodiola Rosea
- Glycine (Heckman, 2019)

Finding Healing During Stress and Grief

You have the power to fight your way through the layers of the cloak of grief. This chapter is full of useful tips and tricks to help you when you start feeling overwhelmed. You don't have to hide. Use the tools you have been given and challenge the boundaries of your comfort zone. Do something you have never done. Put on some music whenever you feel that stress or grief is threatening to suffocate you. Think about all the work you have done to start the healing process before you lose yourself in the bottom of a tub of your favorite ice cream.

You are going to have your ups and downs as you navigate your way through your new normal. Do what you need to do to deal with the loss of your loved ones. Whatever you choose to do should not undermine all the progress you have made towards healing. Working 19 hours a day is not going to benefit you in any way. Eating your emotions is not going to help your body or your immune system. Utilize the tools you have been given to make positive changes. Start small and work yourself up until you know that you are ready to join the mainstream again.

Chapter 6:

Legalities Following the Death of a Loved One

Dare to dream of a perfect world where everyone gets along. The perfect home where families love each other and there is no conflict among siblings or parents. Everyone gets together to celebrate the life of the loved one who has departed from the world. Tears are shed, this one is comforting that one, and everything is fine and dandy in *Mournville*. Well, that bubble popped without any fanfare and glitter bombs. Our worlds may be perfect, but sadly, not everyone lives in that perfect world.

It is sad to think that the world is filled with people who aren't happy with the way their lives are going. They don't hesitate to spew their anger across the various social media platforms. You scroll through their accounts to find the happy memories, but those have all been removed. Unfortunately, people don't get along because of barriers that have been erected for whatever reason. The death of a loved one should strengthen bonds instead of causing irreparable damage because of jealously, greed, or nastiness. Life is way too short to harbor animosity towards anyone, especially family. I wish that I could grab these individuals by their shoulders and make them understand that the death of a loved one is not about who is getting what out of the estate.

Real Life in Your Broken World

This chapter is going to be a little different than what I have discussed thus far. This is an important chapter that may prepare you for the road ahead when dealing with banks, insurances, work, and/or legal issues. There is a side of death that many know about but not many understand. I get that no one wants to think about finances and the legalities involved in the passing of a loved one. Unfortunately, it is a reality, and most of these issues have to be addressed as soon as possible after the passing of your loved one. This is one of those moments where you want to hit the pause button on the remote to make the world stand still for a moment. All you want to do is take a deep breath and allow the reality of your new normal to sink in. Your world will stop, but the rest of the world will continue moving forward.

Before you can properly mourn the loss of your loved one, you are going to have to deal with a whole lot of behind-the-scenes legalities. Not everyone has the opportunity to draw up a last will or even plan their funerals because life is unpredictable. Your loved ones may be around for years after being diagnosed with a disease or they might pass away after being in an accident or suffering a heart attack. No one will ever know when their time on this earth will expire. It would be ideal to have all the ducks in a row, but most times, people don't want to think that far ahead because they believe that they are indestructible. I love a positive person, but I admire someone who thinks of the future. Let's start by taking a look around the legal and financial elements following the death of your loved one.

Bereavement Leave

Are you or are you not entitled to bereavement leave? That is a question that has been asked by many people across the globe. You will receive varied answers depending on where in the world you find yourself. Countries such as Canada, Australia, China, France, and many more offer bereavement leave. What this means is that immediate family members such as children, parents, and spouses are entitled to paid leave anywhere from one to five days for the passing of their loved ones.

Unfortunately, not all countries offer this privilege. The United States is one of those countries that doesn't offer mandatory bereavement leave and it is not part of federal law. It doesn't mean that you can't take time off to mourn the loss of your loved one. In Chapter 1, I cautioned you not to plan for something that is yet to happen. I would like you to take heed of that cautionary warning to stop thinking ahead about something until it is necessary. Speak with your employer. Inform them that your loved one has taken ill so that if and when the time comes, they will be prepared. If you are lucky enough to have an understanding and sympathetic employer, they may just tell you that you could work remotely.

I like to see the good in everyone, even when I lost my job because of the global pandemic. I do like to believe that no one with a heart will deny you the time to spend with your family after the death of a loved one. In fact, most employers will give their employees up to three days of paid leave (possibly more depending on circumstances). Keep the line of communication open with your employers and ask for more time off if you need it. You may be digging into your overtime or vacation days, but it would be worthwhile if it means that you could be on hand to support your immediate family (Greenberg, 2019).

Last Will and Testament

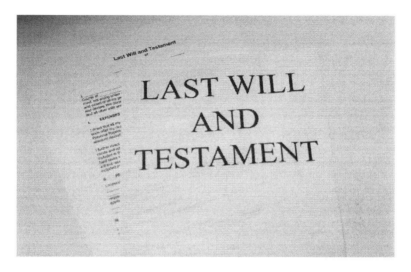

This is where things become a little more intense. Your loved one has been gone for less than a day and you need to rummage through personal effects to find the will or at least a folder with all the necessary documents that are needed upon the death. We were lucky that Dad had appointed Stephen to be the executor of his will. Dad knew what he was doing when he drew up his will and got all his paperwork in order. Not many people have that opportunity. As previously mentioned, many people are living in denial and don't believe in making plans.

We are going to take a little tour around the legalities that form part of having a will. There will be multiple detours as we look at different types of wills and what they should contain. We will gather interesting bits of information that you could put to use when helping your loved one through the process. And then, as much as you would like to believe that everything is sunshine and roses, there may be the slim possibility that complications may arise and a couple of questions:

- What happens if there isn't a will?
- What happens if a family member challenges the will?
- What happens if someone is bequeathed something that has been lost, stolen, given away, or the finances don't allow for those gifts?

I am sure that you have many questions that relate to the will, which I am hoping to shine some light on. I urge you to seek the help of a legal advisor if you have more complex queries. I am not a lawyer. I am sharing what I have learned through my experience with Dad.

Different Types of Wills

Everything you do in life depends on the choices you make. You can be successful if you make the right choices for yourself. You can fail at everything you do if you make choices that are not so smart. Everyone has an opinion when it comes to your life and how you should be living it, but not everyone appreciates being told what they probably shouldn't be doing. You have a couple of options when deciding on the type of will you want. You get the chance to decide which of the options will be the best fit for you and what you require.

Simple Will

The templates for simple wills can be found on the internet by doing a simple search. You get to choose who will get what from your estate such as jewelry, money, and vehicles, as well as appoint a legal guardian for minor children. This will is going to be your last love letter to your loved ones.

Testamentary Trust Will

This type of will is set up to protect your beneficiaries from mishandling their inheritance. You get to appoint a trustee who will oversee that the conditions of the benefactor are met until such time that the beneficiaries have reached the desired age or met the requirements as stipulated. Some people would see this type of will as unnecessary and others would see it as a necessary step, especially if they are going through the poor choices stage of their lives.

Joint Will

These types of wills are typically utilized by married couples. The joint will would look like a simple will. The only difference would be that instead of dispersing items among various beneficiaries, each spouse nominates the other in the event of death. This may seem like a pretty simple solution, but it could lead to problems for the spouse who is left behind. Confused? Here is a little bit of advice for you—always read the fine print. A joint will cannot be changed after the death of a spouse because of the way the will is set out. I would recommend that you seek legal advice if you want to pursue the idea of having a joint will so that the living spouse can make amendments when the time comes.

Living Will

The living will is not about who gets what when you are no longer here. This will help you when you cannot speak for yourself. You get to choose the type of medical treatment you need. This is your chance to let your family know whether you want to be connected to machines to keep your heart beating, your lungs breathing, or tubes to your stomach to keep you nourished. It is your choice. The living will also allows you to appoint someone to make decisions on your behalf.

What a Will Should Look Like

Drawing up a will may seem like a tedious affair, but your loved ones will thank you. You would be dragging out the grieving process if you don't have a will. That would then turn into anger and frustration not related to your death. Everyone needs a will because it doesn't matter what you have in your home, your bank account, or what possessions you own. I'm not going to force you to draw up a will, but it is something to think about, for sure. If Dad didn't have a will, we would never have known he wanted his body donated to science (which we totally botched), and we wouldn't have known what music he wanted to be played at the crematorium. Food for thought.

You will want to do research when drawing up your will because different states have different requirements. What should the body of your will look like? I'm so glad that you asked! Let's take a look at some of the basic information that should be included in your will.

- Your full names.
- Your spouse's name and date of marriage.
- Names of children, whether biological, stepchildren, or foster children.
- A clause revoking all previous wills.
- The name of the person you choose to be the executor of your estate and an alternative name should the first person not be available to help.
- A list of possessions such as property, money, jewelry, art, or gifts you want to leave to specific people.

- A list of instructions for your executor informing them of how to distribute your estates after the financial legalities have been dealt with, such as the settling of debts, paying the taxes, and whatever expenses have been incurred.

Life insurance policies, pension plans, and annuities are not required to be in the will. These types of plans have designated beneficiaries when taken out. It is important to remember that if these plans are mentioned in the will, it will delay the settling of the estate as well as cause tax issues that could have been avoided.

Contesting a Will

Why would anyone want to contest the will of their loved one? Don't believe what you see in the movies or daytime dramas. Not all families are dysfunctional and drama-worthy and there could be a whole host of reasons why a will would be contested. I've already told you what my perfect world looks like, and I have pretty much bared my heart and soul for all to see. I am very close to my family and it doesn't matter that we live more than 4,000 miles apart. We get to speak and see each other every day or even multiple times a day thanks to technology. I do understand that not all families are like mine and it is for that reason that I am covering my bases should you encounter any problems.

Who Is Going to Contest a Will?

Your second cousin twice removed cannot fly in through the doors to contest a will they were named in. Remember, this is not a script written for daytime television. These are real people who have legal rights to challenge the will of a loved one.

- People mentioned in the will.
- People who were mentioned in an earlier will and were excluded from the rewrite for some reason.
- People who believe that their portion of the inheritance was changed to a lesser amount.
- Spouses, children, or next of kin who are not named in legal paperwork because there was never a will.

Legal Reasons to Contest a Will

You need to have a good reason for wanting to contest a will. For familial disputes, you will be required to have proof that the will you are disputing was compromised, invalid, or unfair. It is important to point out that even though you believe you have a strong case, the judge may not agree with your reasoning. There is no way to ask your loved ones why they made the choices they made, and it is something you will have to make peace with. Contesting a will can become a costly and drawn out affair.

In the instance where families are not happy with something about the legalities of the will, they have legal reasons to contest the will. These include reasons that the dearly departed loved one, referred to as the testator:

- Was not mentally competent.
- Was under the undue influence of someone forcing them into changing the will to benefit the beneficiary.

Other legal reasons include:

- The will was not signed by two witnesses.
- Amendments within the document were not signed by two witnesses.
- Inheritance cannot be distributed when a spouse is still alive.
- There should be no evidence of forgery or fraud.
- Knowing that there was a more recent will that had vanished.
- If the will was not completed, such as missing signatures or blank spaces where beneficiaries would have been mentioned.

The Process of Contesting a Will

I am going to caution you, once again, that you will need a legal representative. You need to have an experienced person with you, and no, this is not something you can research on YouTube or use Elle Woods from *Legally Blonde* as your inspiration. You will need an army standing beside you because if you are going to proceed with the contesting, it could become a very costly and lengthy process. Let's take a look at the steps that are needed to start the ball rolling.

- Approach the probate court to submit a claim.
- Start preparing for the hearing.
- Be prepared for an outcome that can go either way and prepare to choose a settlement if things don't go according to the way you want.
- If you win the court case, you will be entitled to take what was originally bequeathed to you.

- If you lose the court case, you will get nothing and you may incur additional costs to cover the costs of the case.

My Story: Part 5

I was very lucky and even blessed as I reflect on how I was raised and the childhood I had. Mum and Dad had been married for 56 years. They had their ups and their downs like any other married couple. Mum and Dad's marriage was firmly bonded together with love. Theirs was a love that I always hoped to experience when it was my turn to marry.

Gillian is five years younger than me and, like any other siblings, we had our differences growing up. There was a whole lot of teasing and fussing, which we would eventually outgrow the older we got. We have some wonderful memories of the times when we did get along. Gillian and I have entered that midlife stage of our lives, and those days of teasing and fussing are collecting dust in the archives. I don't even know if it is possible, but since we've lost Dad, we are even closer.

It dawned on me that this is how a family should be! You realize that you need your family and loved ones close to you when you're being gut-punched by a tragedy or experiencing a dramatic event that reaches into your chest and squeezes your heart. Gillian and I had a wonderful time reminiscing about Dad. We spoke about the good, bad, and sad times. We laughed and cried during the time leading up to the funeral because we could communicate and be there for each other.

It is good to talk, and it is even better to have someone to talk to who understands boundaries. We need alone time, but you also need the comfort only loved ones can give during this time. Gillian and I both helped Mum with the details of the funeral and shared the responsibilities of the arrangements. Dad would have been proud to see us all stand together. No, I *know* that Dad would have been proud. We didn't argue, we didn't disagree on anything, and there was no teasing or fussing.

The important takeaway from this is that you should always stay calm and focused. That is one of the most important steps in the grieving process. Truth be told, you definitely don't need any more drama, because there is only so much a family can deal with. I was incredibly blessed because I had a wonderful upbringing. We have great memories of growing "old" together. I believe that these memories that are filled with love and family are what have made this journey of loss a little more bearable.

Chapter 7:

Messages From the Other Side

Everyone copes with the passing of their loved ones in whatever way they choose. I like to believe that those who have passed away are happy. They are free from baggage they were carrying through life. They don't have to worry or stress about earthly struggles where they are. I may be naïve, but I like to believe that Dad is happy where he is—in heaven—looking down at us from his heavenly perch. Can you imagine the view he has? I mean to say that Mum, Gillian, Stephen, Matthew, and Rosie are in the U.K., and I'm in the United States with Jessica and Alison—that's over 4,000 miles between us. I'm pretty sure that not everyone has the same vision as I do.

Each person interprets the afterlife in a way that pays tribute to their past relationships with their loved ones. You are entitled to believe in whatever you want to help you stay connected with your loved ones. Don't ever let anyone dictate to you what you can and cannot believe in. It is also perfectly fine if you don't believe in the afterlife. Various religious institutions may frown upon your beliefs, and many others speak about joining your loved ones for all eternity. Whatever you believe in is entirely up to you because this may be the Band-Aid that you need to help you cope with the passing of your loved ones.

I am going to take you on another one of my detours where I am going to introduce you to the concept of after-death communication (ADC). I want to dedicate this chapter to those who are struggling to let go of their loved ones. I want to help you look for any signs that you may have missed without realizing it. Your loved ones may have left you some messages to let you know that they are okay. All I am going to ask from you is that you read through this chapter with an open mind. Let down your protective walls and allow yourself to be vulnerable. Take a peek at the light from between the layers of your cloak of grief.

Open Your Heart and Mind

It is not my intention to offend anyone with my beliefs. I would never intentionally mislead others who are experiencing the pain of losing a loved one. I can't even compare what I'm feeling to what everyone else is going through, but I know for sure that we are kindred spirits. We have all experienced a loss so great that we are struggling to put the pieces of our lives back together. It doesn't matter whether you want to numb the pain or if you are looking for closure after the passing of your loved one. No one is going to judge you for seeking out the help of a medium, a psychic, or whichever deity you believe in to help you during this difficult stage of your life.

I don't want to reach the end of the chapter and say that this has been a waste of your time, only to spot one of the signs or messages you have read about. I will share my experience at the end of this chapter and you can decide for yourself what you think about signs or messages. I prepared you for this chapter back in Chapter 4, and I planted many seeds as we traveled along the way. The time is finally here, and I am asking you to open your heart and mind to the possibility that we are surrounded by hidden signs and messages from our loved ones.

Surrounded by Signs

I have heard family, friends, and colleagues talk about experiences they encountered which they could not explain. I have most likely encountered some unexplainable occurrences and never given it much thought. Now that I am on the other side of the grief line, I am putting the pieces together and realizing that maybe, just maybe, my grandparents or my late brother have been sending me messages for many years. Maybe all those face plants on the football field were my brother trying to get my attention. I can't change the past, but I definitely can focus on the future and put my newfound knowledge and information to excellent use.

Butterflies

It is believed that spotting butterflies is one of the most common signs that your loved one is with you. The life cycle of a butterfly occurs in four stages, starting as an egg. The egg hatches and becomes a caterpillar. When the caterpillar has reached the end of his cycle, he becomes a chrysalis until it is time for him to be reborn. The result of the rebirth is a beautiful adult butterfly that breaks out of its pupa and is ready to begin the cycle again. Humans are a lot like butterflies because we started as an egg, we became both the caterpillar and chrysalis while in utero, and then we were born. Okay, so maybe we were not born as adults, but the principles of the life cycles are the same.

Is it any wonder why many cultures believe butterflies are a representation of the human soul and that they symbolize endurance and hope, including the life cycles I have mentioned? There are no coincidences when searching for signs that our loved ones are around us!

Feathers

I am going to go out on a limb and proclaim that I believe that feathers trump butterflies when it comes to signs from the other side. I have heard so many stories about feathers, including my own, that have made the hair on the back of my neck stand up. I came across an expression that adds to my belief about finding feathers: "When feathers appear, angels are near."

The most popular belief among feather finders is that they represent the presence of angels. That is a belief I can get back without a moment's hesitation. I do believe that Dad is an angel, as I know you believe your loved one is an angel, too. I'm not going to tell you that you should go out looking for feathers in your home, garden, or anywhere else you may be. Signs don't work like that. There is a 100% guarantee that you will have feathers if you have a cat.

What is significant about finding special sign feathers is that you will find them in places you wouldn't expect to find them. These feathers will find you if and when the time is right and you are ready. Remember, your loved one knows you better than anyone else, and they will know when to send you a message.

Birds

Certain types of birds are believed to be part of the spirit world that fly in to give you a message that your loved one is with you. It is believed that hummingbirds and cardinals are most commonly reported as the birds that are viewed shortly after the passing of your loved ones. I am partial to believing that doves, pigeons, and red robins are definitely signs that our loved ones are around us.

Dreams

Many believe that our loved ones speak to us in our dreams. I am a little skeptical about dreams. I do believe that our loved ones can send us messages if we are not seeing the signs that they are leaving for us. I do also believe that dreams are a way of living in a make-believe world where our loved ones are still alive.

If you were to ask me about dreams, I would tell you that it is normal to dream about your loved one. I would then tell you to capture all the details of your loved ones and store them in your memory bank. If you are having recurring dreams of your loved ones where they are trying to show or tell you something, then you should take note, because that could very well be a message that they need you to take care of.

More Signs

I have mentioned some of the most common signs that could let you know that your loved ones are around you. The list doesn't end there, and I will give you some more examples of what you could expect in the way of signs and/or messages.

- Unique fragrances that you do not have in your home that are associated with your loved ones, such as perfume or cologne.
- Something you may have been searching for suddenly appears in the exact spot you had searched multiple times before.
- Stones appear in places such as drawers, in pockets, or the middle of the living room floor after you have cleaned.
- Hearing your loved one's voice when you know you are the only one at home or in the car.
- Feeling a brush or a tickle on your face, hand, or arm could be your loved one letting you know that they are right beside you.
- Gut feelings are almost always spot on, and if you sense that your loved one is with you, they most likely are.

Visits From the Other Side

No one can say for sure if, when, or why our loved ones will visit us. Some people would welcome any forms of communication from the afterlife. Many would prefer no visitations. I love visits *and* signs *and* messages, *and* everything else that Dad sends my way. I know that I cannot hold onto him forever and that he is helping us through our grief.

I do believe that visits, signs, and messages are tied to our emotions. You may believe that you are an expert at keeping your emotions under lock and key, but your loved ones know you better. I like to think that they can see straight through us, and because of that, we can't hide things from them the way we could when they were earthbound. Let's take a look at some examples of when they pop in on us and make their presence known. I may have added some examples of signs and visitations during previous chapters, so be sure to go back and read some of the earlier chapters again.

Alone Time

Finding time alone is sacred, scarce, and a luxury no money can buy. Everyone needs some alone time, and it's not just for parents or people who work with others. Alone time is when you have no distractions surrounding you. You may be reading a book, writing in your journal, or listening to the birds chirping in your garden when you start noticing a change in the atmosphere around you. You may feel that brush against your cheek that was mentioned earlier or you might catch a distinctive smell. These are the signs that your loved one has popped in for a visit to let you know that they are doing well and that they love you.

Stressful Situations

It is only natural to want to shut down when you find yourself inundated with a stressful situation. You build up a mental block that doesn't want to deal with the situation but you realize it is something that has to be addressed. It is during these types of situations that your loved ones may pop in to calm the storm in your mind, body, and soul. Don't be afraid to call out for help and guidance. I like to believe that God permits our loved ones to answer our cries for help. We may not physically see them, but we can feel them as they bring calmness with them. You may think that you're alone, but you'll never be alone.

Putting Your Mind at Ease

Please don't feel disheartened, sad, or jealous of those who do receive signs when you don't. It is in no way a reflection on you or the relationship you had with your loved one. They probably know that you are okay and that you are healing the way you should be. They also know that the cloak of grief is not as heavy for you as it is for others in your family. I can almost guarantee that your turn will come when you least expect it, so keep the faith and be patient.

Someone shared a story with me that ties in with this section, which I thought would be appropriate to share with you.

Marsha's grandmother passed away at the age of 95. One Saturday, not too long after her passing, Marsha went to the store to pick up a couple of items. While walking down the produce aisle, tomatoes and lettuce tumbled off the shelf. Marsha looked around to discover that she was the only one in the aisle. She picked up the items and placed them on the shelf and continued down the aisle. As she rounded the corner, the items fell again, but this time, potatoes rolled off the shelf in the new aisle. Again, she went and picked up everything, and instead of returning it to the shelves, she packed them in her shopping cart.

Marsha then continued her shopping and came to the hot beverage aisle. Again, she was alone in the aisle when, out of nowhere, a packet of tea came off the shelf and landed in the cart. At this point, Marsha was having severe anxiety because she was surrounded by glass jars containing coffee: "Okay, Grammy, I get that you are here, but please don't throw any more stuff around!" Marsha didn't bother shopping any further and went to the checkouts so that she could pay and get out. She called her uncle and told him what had happened and he was rather rude because he hadn't had any signs from his mother. He actually put the phone down on her. It wasn't until five months later that her uncle confessed that he had never felt Grammy's presence and he was staying in her apartment.

You see, it doesn't matter who you are or where you are, your loved ones will visit the ones who they believe will share their experience. I think they do this so that the hard-as-nails family members can drop their macho bravado, feel some sensitivity, and experience these signs, messages, and visitations.

My Story: Part 6

The three weeks between Dad's passing and his funeral gave me some time to help Mum with some much-needed admin work. There was so much to do, and I was happy to help Mum. One of the first things I did was go through the accounts. I made a list, almost like a summary, of all the important details such as the utility accounts, bank accounts, passport, and canceling Dad's driver's license that needed to be addressed. I made a separate spreadsheet that detailed all the money coming in from private pension, state pension, and savings. It also showed Mum all the money that was going out to pay the bills. I drew up a budget that gave Mum a rough estimate of how much she would spend on groceries and gas for the car.

I pretty much gave Mum a detailed income and expenditure module that included an expendable income so that she could factor in her shopping budget. Mum loved to go shopping. I showed her what I had done, and she was very happy with the result. It was clear and concise, and, best of all, she didn't need to be an accountant to understand what I had laid out of her.

I created folders for everything Mum would need. Everything was organized, if there were any problems, Mum could easily find the documentation. There was a folder with all the comprehensive details for each of the service providers. Each of the providers had a document that showed the details such as the company name, address, account details, website, and contact number. I wanted everything as user-friendly as possible so that Mum wouldn't become overwhelmed and not know what to do if she had problems with the electricity, for example. She would pull out the folder, find the electricity company's document, and the details needed would be right at her fingertips.

After I had finished sorting through and preparing all the financial documents, I had some free time to help out around the house. One such day, when I was coming down the stairs from my old bedroom, Mum asked me to collect the laundry that was drying on the radiators around the house. Keep in mind, this is in England, and not many people have a clothes dryer. So, as I collected the clothes off the hallway radiator, I found a white feather on the floor. I thought it was odd so I took it to Mum who was making tea in the kitchen. She looked at the feather, then at me, and said, "Oh wow! You know what that means, don't you? That's your dad." I stared at Mum in confusion, not quite understanding the symbolism behind signs yet. Mum explained that finding a white feather is a sign that a loved one that has passed is nearby as an angel.

Needless to say, I was in shock. I had never expected that a feather would mean that Dad was in the same room as me. I choked up thinking about it and wondered if he had tried to reach out to hug me or tell me that he was happy with the way I had simplified the financials for Mum.

Since the first sighting of the white feather, I have found several more during the rest of my stay in the U.K. and after returning to the U.S. It is a precious moment when you see a white feather appear out of nowhere. When it happens, it takes you by surprise to the point where you feel as if you have been winded. It's all the affirmation I need, knowing that Dad is keeping an eye on his family. I've also had dreams about Dad. The dreams are so real that I can still see what he was wearing and I remember every word he said to me. Having these signs, messages, and visits is so surreal but so very welcomed.

Chapter 8:

Finding Comfort in Your Faith or Beliefs After a Loss

I waited until now to bring faith into the picture because I didn't want to force my beliefs onto you. Dealing with the loss of a loved one is not easy. Add in that you will have people telling you to pray and be faithful when your loved one is diagnosed with an incurable disease is something you might not want to hear. Or, that your loved one is in a better place and they are pain-free. Hearing those words is almost as bad as someone telling you that they know what you're going through or that you will get over it.

Religion is a personal choice, and I did not want to influence you or make you feel uncomfortable. I have dropped many hints throughout this book about where I am in my spiritual journey. I want this book to be a safe place where you can find comfort without being pressured when you are going through the stages of grief. I know you are still wrapped up in your cloak of grief, but I would like you to join me on this part of the journey. Let's see what having faith can do for you, me, and whoever else needs it during these trying times.

There will be no brainwashing or subliminal attempts to have you join a cult or any religious institution. This journey is all about making choices that help all fellow grievers. We are like-minded individuals who have one thing in common—the loss of a loved one. I've told you before and I'll tell you again, I have nothing to gain by baring my heart and soul to strangers who are in the same grief boat as me. We have all experienced a loss that pretty much broke us, and I am writing this book to help everyone who's afraid of the feeling they have. You have learned that you cannot put a timeline on grief and there isn't a switch that you can flip to change how you feel. It is a process we all have to go through, and exploring religion is one of those coping mechanisms we need to address.

Finding Faith

Grief can turn you from a continually flowing waterfall to a hot lava-spewing volcano in the blink of an eye. Grief doesn't care whether you are a person of faith or whether you don't believe in anything but your pets. There is no shame when you "lose" your faculties when you go through a traumatic life event such as the death of a loved one. Everyone will feel the same gut-wrenching and agonizing heartache that loss brings.

Have I mentioned that anger is a normal part of the grieving process? You can be angry at everyone, including your loved one and God for turning your world upside down. It is a natural reaction. You spent hours, days, or weeks in prayer when your loved one became ill and you asked God for a miracle. Your pleading and bargaining turned to anger when your loved one passed away. You start questioning your beliefs and you find yourself doubting that God is real. Grief has you looking for someone to shoulder the blame, and who better to pile it up on than the one entity you cannot see?

On the other side of grief, you have people who find peace in their faith. This doesn't mean that you are not feeling the loss of your loved one or that you are numb to the pain it has caused. Putting your faith in God fills you with peace and knowing that one day you will be reunited with your loved one. I heard the following statement from someone who lost their loved one unexpectedly: "God wouldn't have taken my loved one if He didn't think I could cope."

Finding Faith After Loss

You may have put your faith and God on the back burner while you picked up the pieces of your life, but I like to believe that He has got you. He knows that you are hurting and your pain is His. It's okay to feel the way you do, and He doesn't and won't hold it against you. Learn to give yourself a break and know that as much as you want to be alone, God will always carry you, and if you read Chapter 7, you know you are surrounded by angels. You may be wondering how you will know when you're ready to reclaim your faith, or whether you will ever be there again. There is no definitive answer, and the answer depends on where you are in your grieving process. Here are a couple of tips to help you on your road to recovery:

- Don't suppress your grief.
- Pray and talk to God.
- Don't rush the healing process that comes with grief.
- Don't suppress your anger and allow it to consume your every waking moment.
- Allow friends, family, and/0r your community to carry you in their prayers and belief.
- Be at peace and forgive yourself for letting go of your faith until you are ready to return.
- Consider seeking therapy and counseling, or find support groups in your community to help you understand and deal with the loss of your loved one.
- Everything in life happens for a reason, and as cliché as that sounds, it is something worth believing.
- Do something to honor your loved one on significant dates such as having a tattoo done on the anniversary of their passing or planting a rose bush on their birthday.

What Does the Bible Say About the Cloak of Grief?

You may or may not be ready for the spiritual healing and affirmations in this chapter, and that is okay. This chapter will be right here waiting for you when the time is right. The "cloak of grief" has many layers. These layers are made up of all the emotions associated with the loss of loved ones or traumatic life events. No two cloaks are the same, and each cloak is tailored to fit the person to whom it relates. I thought it would be a good idea to backtrack a little and go back in time and space to see what the scriptures say about the layers that make up the cloak of grief.

Anger

Anger is a reactive response when someone says something you may not like. Or, it could be when something doesn't go according to the way you wanted it to go. You may say that you are happy, but your way of speaking or body language tells another story. Anger is something we all struggle with—it is part of our human nature. When you are trying to cope with the anger of losing a loved one, you tend to keep it under wraps. You could be angry with God, your loved one, or yourself for their death. You hold onto your anger and allow it to fester. I do believe that grief and anger are toxic and can cause physical illness.

The best way to release your anger is to address it. If you are angry at God, let Him know. Do what you need to do to release your anger before it overpowers you. Release can take the form of shouting, screaming, ranting, breaking a couple of plates (it could become messy, but it does help), or crying. You do what you need to do to get that pent-up anger out of your body. Be angry with God and demand answers. Granted, you may not get the answers you seek immediately, but keep an eye and an ear out because you will get your answers when you least expect it. You will not be forsaken for anger directed at

God, and He will be with you every step of the way until you are ready to cast your eyes in His direction again.

Seeking Help

The title doesn't scream "layer of grief," but in some ways, it is actually because this layer is cloaked under "pride." Confused? Don't worry. I, too, was confused until someone told me to stop being a gigantic pain in the rear and take a look around me. "If you need help, please ask!" This is another phrase I don't like because when you do ask for help, the excuses start stacking up. You reach a point in your life where you don't want to ask because of the fear of rejection. You erect a wall to protect your pride and ego. You want to be the hero because you believe that you are the glue that is needed to keep everything together.

Delegate and reach out for help. Planning a funeral is a stressful event. Accept help. Your neighbors and community want to help you by making meals, coming in and cleaning up, or taking care of your laundry. Asking for and accepting help from others is your way of honoring God. He didn't intend for us to do everything on our own. It is not a sign of weakness to ask for or accept help from others. God doesn't want us to do everything alone.

Leaning on God for Strength and Support

You are a human being with a heart that beats and sends blood coursing through your veins to all the organs in your body. You are probably rolling your eyes and saying something like, "Wow, thanks for the biology lesson, bright spark." What I am trying to tell you here is that you don't have to be all tough. Let down your protective walls and feel your grief and sadness. Showing emotions is a sign of acceptance, and it also paves the way to healing.

Lean on God and allow Him to carry you during the difficult times you are experiencing. God will always be there for you. You can step off your spiritual path while you are learning to cope with your new normal, and regardless of what anyone tells you, God will be right there beside you. I like to believe that God understands why we are angry, disappointed, and sad after the loss of a loved one. I would like to share a couple of verses to show you what comfort looks like in the bible.

Even though I walk through the darkest valley, I will fear no evil, for you are with me; your rod and your staff, they comfort me. —Psalm 23:4, NIV

For I am convinced that neither death nor life, neither angels nor demons, neither the present nor the future, nor any powers, neither height nor depth, nor anything else in all creation, will be able to separate us from the love of God that is in Christ Jesus our Lord. —Romans 8:38-39, NIV

As a mother comforts her child, so will I comfort you; and you will be comforted over Jerusalem. —Isaiah 66:13, NIV

So do not fear, for I am with you; do not be dismayed, for I am your God. I will strengthen you and help you; I will uphold you with my righteous right hand. —Isaiah 41:10, NIV

Finding Healing in Faith

Now faith is confidence in what we hope for and assurance about what we do not see. —Hebrews 11:1, NIV

You don't need a dictionary to find the meaning of faith when the scripture gives you the perfect definition. Everything we need to heal is found in our faith. It doesn't matter what religion you are or which deity you believe in, as I have previously mentioned; everyone has faith in their beliefs. Yes, I am quoting Christian scripture, but that is because I was born into and raised as a Catholic. This book is a one-size-fits-all type of book that has something for everyone. No one is going to judge your beliefs, and you most definitely won't be victimized or shamed by me for what you do or don't do. As long as you have an outlet and a support system to help you navigate your way through your cloak of grief, you do as you have been doing.

Navigating Grief

I wanted to touch on grief one more time regarding you finding your faith. I would like you to remember that you are not expected to be strong for everyone who has experienced the same loss as you. It doesn't matter if you are older, younger, or the middle child. A loss of a loved one affects the whole family. The grief you feel will be amplified because you are suppressing your feelings to accommodate everyone else's. I have heard from a couple of people that stepping up to be the "stronger" person opens the door to a whole host of problems such as abuse, bullying, or manipulation to get what they want. Stand up and stomp your feet and let everyone know that you suffered a loss as well and that you need to grieve, too. Let's take a look at a couple of verses that will help you deal with your grief.

For we believe that Jesus died and rose again, and so we believe that God will bring with Jesus those who have fallen asleep in him. —1 Thessalonians 4:14

For to me, to live is Christ and to die is gain. —Philippians 1:21

So we fix our eyes not on what is seen, but on what is unseen, since what is seen is temporary, but what is unseen is eternal. —2 Corinthians 4:18

Then I heard a voice from heaven say, "Write this: Blessed are the dead who die in the Lord from now on."

"Yes," says the Spirit, "they will rest from their labor, for their deeds will follow them." —Revelation 14:3

I recently contacted the priest who conducted Dad's funeral, Father Pat, because I needed some spiritual guidance. Dad's first anniversary away was fast approaching, and hot on its heels was the holiday season. It was then when I realized that I needed some spiritual intervention. Father Pat sent me resources in the way of scriptures and prayers to help me through the difficult days. I would like to share one of the prayers that have helped calm my aching heart, and I hope that it will help you:

> I'm praying to you, Lord, to help me fill this huge hole in my heart with your healing light. Please grant me a deeper understanding of your love. Show me ways to build my faith and guide me out of this darkness into your loving light once more. Amen.

My Story: Part 7

We spoke to the funeral home after Dad's funeral and they informed us that it could take up to three weeks for Dad's ashes to be placed into the urn we had chosen. Mum, Gillian, and I had decided that we would each like a small amount of Dad's ashes. The idea was to have it placed in some form of jewelry such as a ring, a pendant, or cufflinks so that we could always have Dad close to us.

I was disappointed that Dad's ashes wouldn't be ready because Alison and I were due to fly back to the U.S. two days after the funeral. That meant that we only had one full day left to be with Mum and the rest of the family. Thereafter, we would be starting our "new" lives without Dad being a physical part of our family.

Imagine my surprise when the funeral home called and told us that Dad's ashes would be ready the very next day! That meant that we could collect Dad on our last day with Mum. It was such a surreal and eerie feeling walking into the funeral home to bring Dad home. The staff was so friendly and very pleasant with us. They had everything ready for us; the ashes, the clothes that Dad wore when he passed away, and the mini keepsake urn boxes. We thanked the staff for all their help and assistance and left with our items.

I was happy that I was still around to go with Mum to the funeral home and support her. Walking into the house, carrying Dad in his new home, was very surreal and somber. Dad was home, in time, to watch over Mum when I left the following day. Always in our hearts and minds, Dad—always and forever. I love you, Dad.

Chapter 9:

Coping With Grief: First Aid

Kit of Supportive Tools

I wanted to dedicate the final leg of our journey together to providing you with a first aid kit. This is not the typical first aid kit that contains Band-Aids, bandages, allergy and pain medication, or burns dressings. This is a virtual first-aid kit where I want to give you the resources you may need to help you navigate your way through your cloak of grief. This kit is going to give you options that are going to help you cope with your emotions and a lot of the "firsts" without your loved ones:

- Your birthday
- Their birthday
- Thanksgiving
- Christmas
- Anniversary
- Wedding
- Grandchild/ren

This is a list that can carry on as you reach milestones—all your firsts. The realization that your loved one is no longer with you can bury you between the layers of the cloak of grief in an instant.

This first aid kit is not designed for coping with the firsts after the passing of your loved one. I wanted to give everyone a comprehensive guide for any stage of the grieving stages or any traumatic stage you may encounter. The world is in turmoil because of the global pandemic that has caused so much damage as it continues in waves. I would love to be the one to tell you that it will be ending soon, but I'm not a liar. Grieving is similar in that the pain you are feeling from the loss of your loved one will be like the ebb and flow of the tides—one day you will feel good and the next you will be overcome with sadness.

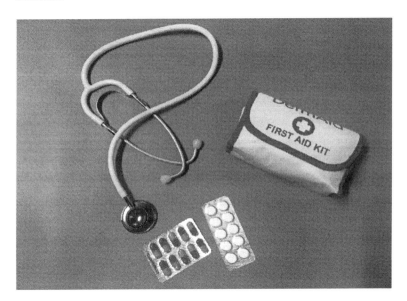

First Aid Kit Inventory

I wanted to put together this first aid kit so that it could help others who are struggling with the loss of a loved one. I know how easy it is to get lost between the layers of the cloak of grief. Imagine that you have been dropped off in the center of a maze and you have to find your way out. After a couple of wrong turns and dead-ends, the lights go out and you are plunged into total darkness. This is what grief is like.

Changing the scenario ever so slightly to where you are put in the center of the maze. You are given a map with helpful information. Now it is time to find your way out of the maze. You hit your first dead-end and realize that you don't want another one and you look at your map. You make it out of the maze before the lights go out because you utilized your map. You avoided the darkness that was threatening to overwhelm you because you had a list of helpful resources.

Let's jump in and take stock of the inventory in your first aid kit. Please note that this is a sample first aid kit and you can customize it to your preferences. And if you were wondering, I will leave you with a "cheat sheet" at the end of the chapter which you can copy, download, or take a photo of to keep in your home, your office, your car, or on your phone.

Grief Counseling

I am not going to be the one that tells you that you have to go for counseling. This is a decision that only the bereaved person can make. Grief counseling offers help to cope with the loss of a loved one. Yes, you can work through the different stages of grief in your own time and there is nothing wrong with that approach. People who should consider counseling are those who struggle to do their daily activities, show signs of depression, carry around a lot of guilt, or struggle to live their lives.

A grief counselor is someone who will use various techniques to help you cope with the loss of your loved one. These counselors are angels because they can help you understand why you feel the way you do, how you can work through your grief, and offer you the support you need. No one can take away the pain you are feeling, but they can give you the tools you need to carry on with your life.

Still not sold on the whole idea of meeting with a grief counselor? Let's take a look at what a typical session would look like. And a little side note, you don't have to talk about anything you aren't comfortable with.

Guilt

You can't change what happened in the past. Your loved one has forgiven you for your mistakes. They will not bring up your past in the afterlife, so why should you hold onto something that they released? Find your peace. Honor your loved one by writing a letter or purchasing a plant. You need to forgive yourself and when you do, your guilt will be washed away.

Remembering Your Loved One

Grief counseling offers you a safe space to talk freely about your loved one. Remember your loved one and reminisce about the good times you had, their favorite movies, books, or music, or anything that you can think of. You don't have to worry about hurting others' feelings when you remember. Remembering your loved one is healing for you.

Dealing With the Dark Side of Grief

Do you remember the dark passages I cautioned you against throughout this book? I think I may have made approximately seven references to those passages. I told you that it is a place you don't want to be, which is why counseling, support, and coping are so incredibly important. Did you know that approximately one million people across the globe take their own lives? Researchers have said that suicide is one of the top three causes of death among all age groups.

Can you imagine how your loved ones would feel if you took your own life? The dark passage is obscuring your path to finding the light because you are harboring many feelings. Those feelings range from feeling confused or rejected to shame or anger because you are still here and your loved one has passed away. The darkness leads you to believe that everyone will be better off without you (Vasquez, 2021).

You may think that you are just another person who walks around and that you won't be missed if you give into your dark thoughts. That passageway has a way of skewing the truth and twisting your feelings to make you believe that there is no place for you. I want to tell you that no matter what you think about yourself, your presence will be missed.

You don't know how many lives you've touched throughout your lifetime. You will never know because you've never thought about the child you helped by reaching an item on a shelf that they couldn't reach. What about the lady who was trying to juggle her shopping cart and stroller? You grabbed her stroller and she couldn't stop thanking you for your help. Oh, and what about the homeless man you walked by who smiled at you? He didn't ask you for anything, yet you gave him $5 to go and buy himself something to eat and drink. Okay, what about the time you were driving along and you saw a car trying to enter from a side road but because the traffic was chaotic, they sat there in despair. You noticed them and you slowed down and flashed your lights to indicate that they could go in front of you.

Do you want to tell me that you won't be missed? You were put on this earth for a reason. Before you take the advice that the dark passageway is giving you, reach out for help. Stay tuned until the end of the chapter when I will have a whole lot of resources to help you deal with your grief.

Cheat Sheet of Helpful Resources

I have put together a list of helpful resources to help you through the loss of your loved one. You can take a photo or screenshot to either keep on your phone or print it out and have them lying around for yourself or others who may need help but are afraid to ask. I have added contact numbers, websites, social media handles, and whatever else I thought would be appropriate for your first aid kit and resource list.

Grief Counseling	Suicide Prevention
https://www.psychologytoday.com/us/therapists	United States of America National Suicide Prevention Lifeline https://suicidepreventionlifeline.org/ 1 800 273 8255
https://www.psychologytoday.com/ca/therapists	Canada The Canada Suicide Prevention Service https://www.crisisservicescanada.ca/en/ 1 800 456 4566
https://www.psychologytod	The United Kingdom

ay.com/gb/counselling	National Suicide Prevention Helpline UK https://www.spbristol.org/N SPHUK 0800 689 5652

Support Groups	
Facebook:	**Twitter:**
• Grief Speaks Out https://www.facebook.com/GriefSpeaksOut • Grief in Common https://www.facebook.com/griefincommon • Grief Anonymous Family Hub https://www.facebook.com/groups/GriefAnonymousFamily	• @HealGrief https://twitter.com/healgrief • @ModernLoss https://twitter.com/modernloss • @GriefSpeaks https://twitter.com/griefspeaks • @GriefRecovery https://twitter.com/griefrecovery
Instagram:	**TikTok:**
• @refugeingrief https://www.instagram.com/refugeingrief/ • @going_with_grace https://www.instagram.com/going_with_grace/ • @findmywellbeing	• @lindsay.fleminglpc https://www.tiktok.com/@lindsay.fleminglpc? • @selfcare.hugs https://www.tiktok.com/@selfcare.hugs? • @amoderntherapist

	https://www.tiktok.com/@a moderntherapist?
https://www.instagram.com /findmywellbeing/ ● @howmental https://www.instagram.com /howmental/ ● @letsreimagine https://www.instagram.com /letsreimagine/	
Grief and Support Forums	**Self-Care Tips**
● https://www.grieving.com ● https://www.griefhealingdiscussiongroups.com/ ● https://www.griefincommon.com/ ● http://www.onlinegriefsupport.com/forum ● https://mysupportforums.org/grief-and-loss/ ● http://connect.legacy.com/inspire/grief-support-community-1 ● https://www.joincake.com/forum/	● Journaling ● Don't push people away ● Accept all help when offered ● Surround yourself with positive people ● Spend time in prayer ● Find your faith when the time is right ● You can smile, laugh, joke, and grieve without judgment

Conclusion

We've reached the part of the book you're either happy to see the end of or sad because you want more. I would love to carry on and share so much more of my experiences with you, but I have to release you. There comes a time when all good things have to come to an end.

I have taken you on a tour where you were introduced to the cloak of grief and its many layers. Your journey has had its ups and its downs. Travel journeys are never as smooth-going as people make them out to be; a road trip could have you hitting every pothole from here to Timbuktu, a plane ride could have you hitting turbulence, or a trip on a cruise-liner would most likely have you tossing biscuits because of the rocking waters.

Real-life journeys are bound to toss you a couple of curveballs and roadblocks on the way to finding yourself. Everyone needs to get to their destination at some point. It doesn't matter what you went through yesterday, what you're going through today, or what you're going to be going through tomorrow; there are no guarantees for the outcome. Deal with your grief the way you feel comfortable, but don't do it alone. I recently read something that was published on the Newspring Church in Anderson, South Carolina's website that I wanted to share with you. I kept it for the conclusion because I believe that it summarizes grief in a way that will make you understand the process a little better. They mention that struggling to cope with grief is like "swimming in a pool of peanut butter" (Marshall, 2015).

My Story: The End

I suffered from lots of headaches in the days after the loss of
Dad. I've managed to keep living in the new normal. The pain
and grief of losing Dad hasn't been easy to apply to my new
normal, and the cracks threaten to show themselves every so
often. I have learned to adjust my way of thinking and
participate in activities that are beneficial to my health and well-
being. I'll take a walk around the local lake or sit in the
backyard and watch the birds look for food or the bees
collecting pollen. I'd take naps in the morning or afternoon to
help clear the fog that threatens to fill my mind, as well as keep
my attitude in check—that cuff on the ear from the heavenly
perch is a constant reminder.

I never know when I'm going to be overcome by grief or how severe the feelings are going to be. I had to learn to adopt new methods to help me because this was all part of my new normal. I have started exercising again and I have been riding my bike to keep the cortisol levels at an even keel. Being able to exercise has also helped me clear my head.

I'll never put Dad in the past. I'll scoot him, ever so gently, to the side so that he can be with me. That way, we'll always be together and I can walk through the rest of my life with the bravest man I have ever known. Dad, "You'll Never Walk Alone," because Mum, Gillian, and I will be there until the day you bring us to you. Thank you for allowing me to share your memory with strangers who have yet to meet you when they pass through the pearly gates.

May your God go with you.

References

10 Things you can do when you're stressed. (2019, September 9). Mental Health America. https://www.mhanational.org/blog/10-things-you-can-do-when-youre-stressed

Adikwu, M. (2020, August 22). *What is grief counseling and how does it help?* Talkspace. https://www.talkspace.com/blog/grief-counseling-therapy-definition-what-is/

American Psychological Association. (2020, January 1). *Grief: Coping with the loss of your loved one.* American Psychological Association. https://www.apa.org/topics/families/grief

Anas, B. (2018, December 6). *Here's how grief affects both our minds and bodies.* Simplemost. https://www.simplemost.com/how-grief-affects-both-our-minds-and-bodies/

Bible verses about grief. (n.d.). Keepsakes Etc. https://www.keepsakes-etc.com/grief-bible-versus.html#Bible_Verses_About_Grieving_Death_

Biblegateway. (1993). *A searchable online bible in over 150 versions and 50 languages.* Biblegateway. https://www.biblegateway.com/

Bruce, D. F. (2021, June 28). *When sadness becomes clinical depression: Signs to look for.* WebMD. https://www.webmd.com/depression/guide/what-is-depression#091e9c5e800090de-2-6

Bryant, C. W. (2007, November 30). *How wills work.* HowStuffWorks. https://money.howstuffworks.com/personal-finance/financial-planning/will.htm

Campbell, J. (2018, March 18). *How to write a eulogy.* Legacy. https://www.legacy.com/advice/how-to-write-a-eulogy

Caraballo, S., & Hurwitz, K. (2021, January 8). *What does the bible say about anger? Here are 15 verses to guide you.* Woman's Day. https://www.womansday.com/life/inspirational-stories/g29328885/bible-verses-about-anger/

Carey, I. M., Shah, S. M., DeWilde, S., Harris, T., Victor, C. R., & Cook, D. G. (2014). Increased Risk of Acute Cardiovascular Events After Partner Bereavement. *JAMA Internal Medicine, 174(4),* 598. https://doi.org/10.1001/jamainternmed.2013.14558

Crisis Services Canada. (2019, December 15). Crisis Services Canada. https://www.crisisservicescanada.ca/en/

Crowther, L. (2019, April 20). *How to help a grieving parent.* Legacy. https://www.legacy.com/news/how-to-help-your-grieving-parent-and-yourself-after-the-death-of-your-mom-or-dad/

Eat these foods to reduce stress and anxiety. (2021, June 15). Health Essentials from Cleveland Clinic.

https://health.clevelandclinic.org/eat-these-foods-to-reduce-stress-and-anxiety/

Fairchild, M. (2021, January 6). *Learn the meaning of faith as defined in the bible.* Learn Religions. https://www.learnreligions.com/what-is-the-meaning-of-faith-700722

Funeral leave | U.S. Department of Labor. (n.d.). Www.dol.gov. https://www.dol.gov/general/topic/benefits-leave/funeral-leave

Greenberg, E. (2019, August 21). *Bereavement leave around the world.* Papaya Global. https://papayaglobal.com/blog/bereavement-leave-around-the-world/

Gregory, C. (2016). *Five stages of grief - understanding the Kubler-Ross model.* Mental Health Treatment Resource since 1986. https://www.psycom.net/depression.central.grief.html

Heckman, W. (2019, November 21). *7 Best vitamins and supplements to combat stress.* The American Institute of Stress. https://www.stress.org/7-best-vitamins-and-supplements-to-combat-stress

Hertzenberg, S. (n.d.). *Can Christians be angry with God when people die?* Beliefnet. https://www.beliefnet.com/love-family/life-events/can-christians-be-angry-with-god-when-people-die.aspx

Hoeppner, A. (2015, October 1). *Three reasons why asking for help is honoring to God.* Unlocking the Bible. https://unlockingthebible.org/2015/10/three-reasons-why-asking-for-help-is-honoring-to-god/

How to do welcome greetings at a funeral service? (2019, July 12). That Flower Shop. https://www.thatflowershop.co/how-to-do-welcome-greetings-at-a-funeral-service/

Johnson, J. (2013, July 29). *The top 5 things to do when a loved one is dying.* HuffPost. https://www.huffpost.com/entry/death-of-a-loved-one_b_3668193

Jon. (n.d.). *The day of the funeral - Funeral Advice.* Funeral Advice. https://www.funeraladvice.org/the-day-of-the-funeral/

Kaminsky, M. (2021, July 22). *What are the 4 types of wills and what should they include?* Legalzoom. https://www.legalzoom.com/articles/what-are-the-4-types-of-wills-and-what-should-they-include

Kessler, S. (2021, November 8). *10 Popular claims of signs from deceased loved ones | Cake Blog.* Cake Blog. https://www.joincake.com/blog/signs-from-deceased-loved-ones/

Marshall, B. (2015, November 25). *12 Things I wish someone had told me about grief.* NewSpring Church. https://newspring.cc/articles/12-things-i-wish-someone-had-told-me-about-grief

McLeod, B. (2021, February 7). *21 Comforting bible verses for funerals | Cake Blog.* Cake Blog. https://www.joincake.com/blog/bible-verses-for-funerals/

Meder, A. (2014a, January 27). *10 Most common signs from your deceased loved ones.* Amanda Linette Meder. https://www.amandalinettemeder.com/blog/2014/1/27/10-signs-from-your-deceased-loved-ones

Meder, A. (2014b, February 6). *When do spirits stop by? The 4 most common visitation times.* Amanda Linette Meder. https://www.amandalinettemeder.com/blog/visitation s-from-your-deceased-loved-ones

National Suicide Prevention Helpline UK - 0800 689 5652. (n.d.). Suicide Prevention Bristol. https://www.spbristol.org/NSPHUK

National Suicide Prevention Lifeline. (2019). National suicide prevention lifeline. Lifeline. https://suicidepreventionlifeline.org/

Quotes - you take the blue pill [...] you take the red pill. (n.d.). Shmoop. https://www.shmoop.com/quotes/you-take-the-blue-pill-you-take-the-red-pill.html

Segal, S. (2017, July 25). *How to write an unforgettable obituary.* Legacy. https://www.legacy.com/advice/how-to-write-an-unforgettable-obituary/

Sigel, Z., & Suh, E. (2021, November 2). *Contesting a will: How to contest a will and why.* Policygenius. https://www.policygenius.com/wills/contesting-a-will/

Tal Young, I., Iglewicz, A., Glorioso, D., Lanouette, N., Seay, K., Ilapakurti, M., & Zisook, S. (2012). Suicide bereavement and complicated grief. *Dialogues in Clinical Neuroscience, 14(2),* 177–186. https://www.ncbi.nlm.nih.gov/pmc/articles/PMC3384 446/

The funeral reception. (n.d.). Funeralwise. https://www.funeralwise.com/celebration-of-life/reception/

Vasquez, Dr. A. (2021a, May 20). *What can you do if you lose faith after a loved one dies? | Cake Blog.* Cake Blog. https://www.joincake.com/blog/losing-faith-in-god-after-someone-dies/

Vasquez, Dr. A. (2021b, October 1). *How to recognize your grief triggers: Step-By-Step | Cake Blog.* Cake Blog. https://www.joincake.com/blog/grief-triggers/

What to expect at a post-funeral reception. (n.d.). Everplans. https://www.everplans.com/articles/what-to-expect-at-a-post-funeral-reception

What to expect the day of a funeral. (2012, November 27). Funeral Blog. https://www.imortuary.com/blog/what-to-expect-the-day-of-a-funeral/

All images sourced from unsplash.com.

All Bible verses are taken from the New International Version (NIV).